THE
SCIENTIFIC THEIST

THE SCIENTIFIC THEIST

A LIFE
OF FRANCIS ELLINGWOOD ABBOT

BY
SYDNEY E. AHLSTROM

AND
ROBERT BRUCE MULLIN

ISBN 0-86554-236-8

The Scientific Theist
Copyright © 1987
Mercer University Press, Macon, Georgia 31207
All rights reserved
Printed in the United States of America

The paper used in this publication meets
the minimum requirements of American National Standard
for Information Sciences—Permanence of Paper
for Printed Library Materials, ANSI Z39.48-1984.
∞™

Library of Congress Cataloging-in-Publication Data
Ahlstrom, Sydney E.
The scientific theist.

"Based on Sydney Ahlstrom's Harvard dissertation of
1951"—Pref.
Bibliography: p.156
1. Abbot, Francis Ellingwood, 1836-1903.
2. Philosophers—United States—Biography.
3. Unitarians—United States—Biography.
4. Rationalists—United States—Biography.
I. Mullin, Robert Bruce.   II. Title.
B945.A264A73   1987   210'.92'4   86-33128
ISBN 0-86554-236-8 (alk. paper)

CONTENTS

PREFACE

Some historical figures are studied because of the belief that their lives and careers embody their respective ages. We speak confidently of an "age of Pericles" or an "age of Jackson." If this were the only reason for biography, Francis Ellingwood Abbot would merit little more than a footnote. He is remembered chiefly (when he is remembered at all) as an advocate of Free Religion, a militant critic of Christianity, secularist, and positivistic evolutionary philosopher. His "age," conversely, is remembered for its lush Victorian sentimental piety, its concern to direct the course of the Republic by the principles of evangelical Christianity, and a growing interest in philosophical idealism. Few individuals were more out of step with their age than Abbot was with the world of late-nineteenth-century America. To any student of popular movements he must appear as an oddity at best, an aberration at worst.

Other figures, however, derive their significance precisely through being at odds with their contemporaries, and in the case of Abbot the antithesis between his life and thought and that of his age opens a window into the epoch. The last third of the nineteenth century was a period of intellectual and cultural uncertainty lurking behind the confident face of Victorian optimism. Many of the most fundamental questions and problems of the era—the reconciliation of science and religion, reason and revelation, morality, and freedom—were all too often glossed over through a combination of sentimentality, philosophical idealism, and decorum. A number of men and women were unwilling to sidestep the central issues of the era, and so became in their own terms "radicals." A study of the life of Abbot is necessarily also an account of this intellectual subculture composed of anti-Christian Unitarians and Reform Jews, scientific philosophers, spiritualists, and freethinkers generally. Whatever internal disagreements these radicals might have had (and Abbot assiduously searched all of these out), as a group they found themselves cultural and psychological outcasts from the warm world of postbellum America. As a representative figure of Victorian religious radicalism, Abbot presents an essential perspective for understanding the period.

What makes Abbot's life so interesting is that he was more than this. He was not merely a chronicler of his age, nor simply a critic, but in his inmost soul a product and, one might almost say, a casualty of his age. Both as a public figure and a private figure Abbot wrestled with questions that bedeviled many of his generation. He was a child of proper Boston Unitarianism, trained at the citadels of the "Unitarian conscience" such as the Boston Latin School and Harvard College. No one reflected better than Abbot the assumptions of morality, order, and sober piety—tempered by the poetic spirit of romanticism—that constituted the world of antebellum Unitarianism. Yet in the space of a decade his well-constructed religious world crumbled and he found himself facing the great void of the post-Darwinian universe. As with so many of his generation, his religious faith was shaken by the question of science. Abbot graduated from college in the year that Charles Darwin's *Origin of Species* was published, and the problem of finding a place for religion in a world of science became an overriding consideration for him. Neither traditional Unitarianism nor even Transcendentalism would suffice anymore. Through this crisis he became one of the earliest theological advocates of evolutionary doctrine. The same crisis that led some to agnosticism and others to reconfirmed belief forced Abbot in a fundamentally different direction. Only by grounding religion in the new scientific method could it again be anchored in truth. By the end of the 1860s he was convinced that the only way to preserve religion was to sever it from its superstitious base, which included Christianity itself.

By studying Abbot one can also gain a better understanding of what it meant during the last third of the nineteenth century to be a radical. Abbot, for example, was a devotee of Ralph Waldo Emerson but a sharp critic of Transcendentalism. He was a secularist liberal who supported the censorship campaign of Anthony Comstock. No aspect of his life was left untouched by his great need to rediscover a ground of certainty in which truth and liberty might again meet. Indeed, one of the most interesting aspects of Abbot's life was his attempt to apply his principles to the social sphere in the great debates of the 1870s. As a staunch proponent of the National Liberal League's secularist vision and campaigns in opposing evangelical attempts to shape national policy, Abbot may be viewed as one of the early advocates of a "post-Christian America." Yet Abbot never ignored the question of how one anchored a public morality in such a world, and in the "free love" debates of the 1870s he attempted to draw some line between liberals and libertines. Finally, the life of Abbot is also the continuing attempt to find in philosophy what had been lost to traditional theology because of the theory of evolution—a grounding of reason, truth, and reality. Even here, however, Abbot's "solution" set him bitterly at odds with the reigning American philosophical schools.

Finally, by examining Abbot one may glean important insight into the transformation of American Unitarianism from a professedly Christian community to its present pluralistic state. Though Abbot and the radicals were defeated in the "Battle of Syracuse," the questions they raised concerning the constrictive nature of even the liberal Christianity of Channing Unitarianism were ultimately to have a strong effect upon the later course of that community. The Free Religious movement spurred the search for a religion freed from revelation.

As in any biography, all of these public questions are mediated through an individual personality. A public history of Abbot without some hint of his inner turmoil would not merely be flat, it would also be unrealistic. Throughout the debates over the direction of Unitarianism, the "religious" amendment to the Constitution, and Kantian philosophy Abbot's peculiar personality comes through—agonizingly serious, humorless, and self-assured. The stories of Abbot's personal life and public life contain the same themes: great potential, moments of hope, yet an ultimate sense of frustration. A number of factors contributed to this sense of failure, but for the student of history Abbot's failure is as illuminative as a dozen other individuals' success.

This work is based on Sydney Ahlstrom's Harvard dissertation of 1951. In the spring of 1983 we began to look at it and were amazed how well it had weathered the years. Furthermore, the events of the early 1980s made it clear that the religious issue of Darwinism, the question of a "Christian America," and the problem of obscenity and censorship were by no means arcane issues of the nineteenth century. In the year that followed we rewrote (and significantly shortened) the original dissertation, refocusing the original study in order to emphasize the contextuality of Abbot's life. The death of Sydney in the summer of 1984 only created an added impetus to finish the revisions. The present text is largely the work of that recasting.

Both Yale University, through its A. Whitney Griswold faculty research fund, and the School of Humanities and Social Sciences of North Carolina State University, by means of a publication subvention grant, have supported this project and have helped it reach completion. Their generosity has been greatly appreciated.

Furthermore, in the completion of this project the help of others must be acknowledged. From the *Proceedings* of the Unitarian Historical Society we were given gracious permission to include a part of chapter 5 that was originally published in that journal (18:2 [1973-1975]: 1-21). Ms. Ann Rives and Ms. Adea Allen of the secretarial staff of the Department of Philosophy and Religion, North Carolina State University, have helped in the final preparation of the manuscript. Finally, a special thanks must be offered to Ms. Laurie Maffley-Kipp, one of Sydney's last graduate students, who did innumerable labors to make this a better work.

CHAPTER ONE

A Boston Boy

ON 6 NOVEMBER 1836, on Beacon Hill, at the corner of Mount Vernon and Joy streets, a third son was born to Joseph Hale and Fanny Ellingwood Abbot. Few other places could have been less auspicious for the birthplace of one of the most infamous religious radicals of the nineteenth century than the proper confines of Beacon Hill, yet it was there that Francis Ellingwood Abbot first saw the light of day.

There had been Abbots in New England from almost the very beginning of the colony. For two centuries the descendants of George Abbot had farmed, taught, and preached, but in whatever calling they had been New Englanders with a strong sense of rectitude and piety as well as champions of learning, freedom, and religious liberalism. It was a heritage Frank could always be proud of: "I am a Puritan of the Puritans," he would boast. And no one represented these virtues as well as Joseph Hale Abbot. A marginally successful schoolmaster with scientific interests, he seemed to personify the old New England values of intellectual rigor, moral purity, social stability, righteousness, and order. "I have never used an obscene or profane word," he announced when he was more than sixty, "nor ever had the desire to." Everything for the senior Abbot had a place; work was to go according to schedule, and there were rules for the conduct of life. These rules were religiously reflected in the staunch Unitarianism of the "Channing/Norton" school, with its almost stoical view of ethical propriety.

What a contrast, however, was Fanny Ellingwood Abbot, especially in the realm of religion. Hers was the soul of a poet, more at home in the arena of nature than in the pedantic schoolroom of her husband. During the lonely summer months of her youth she recalled that she had learned to "commune with nature." "It was here," Abbot's mother said, "that my soul grew." Throughout her life she revealed these predilections in her literary preferences and in her maternal counsels, with the central theme of both being: the world told God's glory.[1]

---

[1]These observations about the character of Abbot's parents are taken from

No biography of Francis Ellingwood Abbot can avoid mention of the imposing contrasts between these two individuals, especially since much of Frank's public life and almost all of his private life was played out between these differences. From the first Frank seemed more the child of his mother. As a child he was not robust. Remembering an incident when Frank was fourteen, his father spoke of "the invalid boy" while his mother referred to him as her "pale little scholar." How much of this tendency was actually created or accentuated by the extreme fears of his father, who always dreaded illness, there is no way of telling. In any event Frank was brought up according to a strict regimen, with required walks in the Boston Common "for exercise" and he was not allowed to participate in most activities of boys his own age. The headaches that racked his adult years began early. Scarcely a week passed without an indication of them in his youthful diaries. Due to his frail health and because his parents felt that he would fare better by being taught at home, Frank was not sent to school until 1851, at which time he entered Boston Latin School.[2]

The keynote of the Abbot household was seriousness. His two older brothers, Henry and Edwin, were mature for their ages and parental in their attitude toward the younger members of the family. Henry, "by right of the strongest," required Frank to feed their pet rabbit and take daily exercise in the park. Henry also made a chart to tabulate Frank's performance, and thrashed Frank more than once for being remiss in his duties. Their parents, moreover, believed in making the most of time. Soon the "infant sports" that had made memories of the early years on beautiful Mount Vernon Street so pleasant gave way to more earnest business. Opportunities for play were limited, and his typical schedule as a fourteen-year-old was highly utilitarian: "I generally get up, eat my breakfast, do the errands after prayers [the errands were many, and often took several hours] and then study the rest of the forenoon. Afternoon, sometimes study, and sometimes go out with Mother. In the evening I sometimes write, and sometimes read till about nine or ten, and then go to bed." Even "entertainment" tended to be serious: lectures, concerts, and a few of the better plays.

---

late entries in Francis Ellingwood Abbot's (hereinafter referred to as FEA) College Diary, 13 and 31 October 1875. There were six Abbot children in all: Henry Larcom (b. 1831), Edwin Hale (b. 1834), Francis Ellingwood (b. 1836), Emily Frances (b. 1839), Edward Stanley (b. 1841), and William Fitzhale (b. 1853).

[2]John Witt Randall, *Poems of Nature and Life,* intro. Francis Ellingwood Abbot (Boston, 1899) 70. Hereinafter referred to as Abbot, "Randall."

Attendance at these, as well as most of Frank's other social inter-course, was with his elders. As was true of Henry Adams during these same years, Frank would, until reluctantly sent to bed, be a constant and absorbed listener of the serious discussions that were held in his father's study until long after midnight.[3]

Religion contributed much to this air of seriousness. Ephraim Peabody, their minister at King's Chapel and a close friend, was not one to minimize the devotional aspects of the religious life. Prayers followed breakfast, and the Sabbath was rigorously observed with services in the morning and suitable reading or memory work in the afternoon. Frank's first journal, kept for a visit to Martha's Vineyard in 1845, reveals an eight-year-old already critical of sermons: "I went to church in the forenoon," he wrote in a childish scrawl, "and thought to myself this is not half so good as Mr. Putnam at home."[4]

Education was in the foreground of the Abbot household. Even daily walks were put to instructive purposes. The children went from baby toys to the three R's, with their father supervising and their mother conducting the daily routine. The process was not dull—for Emily, his sister, later remembered how much fun it had been for them "to go to school" in the home. And this process was thorough; Frank was reading widely and writing with a fine stylistic sense before his twelfth year. Even during summer holidays most of the morning was devoted to "school" and a clearly defined portion of the afternoon to "lessons." During visits away from home, Frank would be enjoined by his mother to study as much as he could, while his father would insist on Latin exercises.[5]

Yet it would be a serious distortion to present the boy's childhood as one consisting of only lessons, errands, and supervised obser-vances. Diametrically opposed to the drill and instruction was his mother's poetic temperament. The two older boys became in many respects replicas of their father, since they were hard-headed, prac-tical men of affairs; but the other three, particularly Frank, became both by inheritance and by influence more as their mother was. "Frank was always the dreamer," his cousin once remarked. By the time

[3]Ibid., 52; Diary, 16 April 1851.

[4]August 1845, third day of Journal. George Putnam was minister of the (Unitarian) First Church of Roxbury and sometime editor of the *Christian Examiner,* a Unitarian journal.

[5]See, e.g., Diary, 4 June 1851; Mother to FEA, 25 September 1848 and 23 September 1850; Father to FEA, 4 August 1851.

Frank was eight his Aunt Sarah perceived his "quiet-gentle spirit." Aspirations to become a poet appeared on the boy's horizon at an early age; and he remembered himself as "a solitary child whose whole playtime went to scribblings of his own, chiefly in rhyme."[6]

Fanny Abbot inspired the young boy profoundly. She awakened his responsiveness to poetry when he was thirteen by reading Sir Walter Scott's *Lay of the Last Minstrel* to him. That same summer (1850) he was deep in Marmion and admiring Sir Walter Scott "more than any other author I ever read." His mother also patiently encouraged him when Frank tried his own hand at writing. "God bless her! God bless her!" he wrote in his college diary, "If I ever become a poet, I will always attribute it all to thee, oh my mother." It was appropriate, therefore, that Frank addressed his first "lyric" to his mother. For the sake of domestic tranquility, Fanny Abbot had him address it to his father, who was coming home to Beverly from teaching in Boston that July evening in 1850. The imperfections of its meter are not nearly so significant as the dolorous note the poet was sounding so early in life.

> Dearest Father, thee I love,
> Better than my tongue can tell;
> May all blessings from above,
> Fall on thee, and keep thee well.
>
> If e'er on thee the storm should fall,
> And all around seem dark and drear,
> May God be unto thee a wall,
> And shelter, so thou shalt not fear.
>
> When on thy deathbed thou dost lie,
> And round thee thou dost hear our sighs,
> May God to thee be ever nigh,
> And take thee to him in the skies.[7]

The poem that Frank wrote for his mother on the following New Year's Day proved good enough to win the English poetry prize at the Latin School, a feat no other first-year boy had ever accomplished. A year later Frank was sending poetry to his father in hopes that a publisher would be found.

_____

[6]See College Diary, 31 October 1875 (a late entry); Diary, 26 January 1879 (quoting Mary Susan Everett); Sarah Abbot to FEA, 15 April 1856; Abbot, "Randall," 70.

[7]Diary, 29 July 1850, 16 December 1855; the poem is found in Childhood Papers.

Frank as a young boy was seriously hampered by a stammer. This stammer was another reason for not sending him off to school, but explaining this problem is not so simple. Could a sensitive, precocious boy, caught between his mother's rule of love and his father's rule of discipline, reconcile the conflicts he faced? Henry, the oldest, went to West Point and became a major general while Edwin became a corporate lawyer; Emily, who was closest in age to Frank, was an apostle of the heart, and by virtue of her sex this yielded fewer problems. Stanley died while still a young man and William grew up almost entirely under his mother's guidance. Thus the full brunt of parental incompatibility fell upon Frank; only in him were both principles strong. Perhaps this explains why this speech impediment remained unresolved to his death. After going away to college, Frank was able to overcome the stammer for the most part; however, it continued to make him wary of extemporaneous speaking, and for certain sounds it was always noticeable.

Dolor and melancholy were far from the only elements of Frank's childhood experience. There was good reason why he should look back nostalgically to "the days when we were little children, and when I, at least, had none of those bitter remembrances, bitter from their very sweetness to poison my peace my mind." Puritan austerity was not carried to such an extreme that the children were kept from dancing school. Nor were the children denied nights for visiting older friends, which could become lively occasions, memorable for stories, music, games, and dancing. Frank also took music lessons. The training never resulted in any great proficiency, but it provided a basis for endless childhood hours at the melodeon, some guitar playing while at college, and a lifetime interest in concert music. In the summer of 1850 he even took to composing although these efforts—perhaps providentially—have not been preserved.[8]

The most important diversions from the constraints at home were the summers in Beverly where Frank enjoyed some measure of freedom and had playmates of his own age. The seashore and his grandfather's barn or workshop provided endless opportunities for adventuring, craftsmanship, or, as he said, *otium cum dignitate*. The shorter visits to relatives in Wilton, New Hampshire, were even more broadening. He often was sent there for several months at a time. Frank usually visited in the autumn with the hope that outdoor work and play "in the pure and bracing atmosphere" would make him well

---

[8]Abbot, "Randall," 52; Diary, 30 April 1851.

and strong. "I am getting to be a complete horseman," he wrote in 1848; only a few days before, he had been paid the signal honor of being entrusted to take the horse and wagon to the village "alone." No wonder he would cry when the time came to leave.[9]

These rural visits also brought Frank closer to nature as well as teaching him lessons he never forgot. The words that Frank was to speak to his future wife, though designed outwardly to explain her feelings, were thoroughly autobiographical.

> When you were little . . . you had an undefinable longing which you did not understand, but which made you unhappy. You went with other children, but you felt they were not like you at all, although doubtless you loved many of them. As you grew older, you used to go alone into the fields and woods, and stay out there a long time; when you were with Nature, you forgot this unspoken and almost blind feeling of loneliness. You used to watch the sunsets, and gaze into the river, and pore over the flowers, and find a sweet solace in their companionship; at those times you felt very happy.[10]

The person who guided the boy to a deeper appreciation of nature was John Randall. Frank felt that Randall was "my first friend outside of my own family . . . the one friend of my boyhood . . . the man of genius, the recluse, the sternest will and the tenderest heart in the world . . . who taught me the beauty and joy of a romantic friendship in my boyhood." To the pale and somber boy this eccentric bachelor was a deliverer. Randall (1813-1892) had graduated from Harvard in 1834. Following the profession of his father, Randall then went on to complete his medical training but never practiced medicine. John Randall was a naturalist by inclination; his researches and his accomplishments in various branches of natural history were painstaking. He was also an avid reader, an amateur poet, and a collector of engravings. In all of these endeavors Randall published little, as he had a sincere desire for anonymity. Randall was a man, as he said, who "was impressed with the conviction how inferior are our artificial pleasures to those simple enjoyments of wood, water, air, and sunshine, which we have unconsciously and inexpensively in common

---

[9]Mother to FEA, 23 September 1850, 6 September 1858; FEA to Mother, 17 and 18 September 1848.

[10]Diary, 12 May 1857.

with the innumerable creatures equally capable of enjoying them."[11] In college and afterward he was known as a solitary man, odd in both manner and dress but remarkable as an observer and sympathetic by nature. Randall never married and lived most of his life with his two talented sisters, Anna and Belinda; and he made the improvement of their country estate near Stow, Massachusetts, a major occupation.

Randall's religious views were not orthodox despite the staunch Unitarianism of his father and his sisters' loyalty to the Reverend Edward Everett Hale. His "Ode to God" is a restatement of the usual tenets of natural religion; but a longer work, "The Philosopher in Search of a Religion," is more pertinent to Abbot's development. This longer work states the dilemma posed by the comparative religionists and then relates "the horrid tale" of religions in "the dark page of history." The great ethical injunctions of the Bible are praised, but ultimately the poem settles into a pessimistic, slightly awestruck agnosticism.

> How passing small
> Man's works! How weak his passions, vain his troubles!
> Earth, sun, moon, stars, the heavens, mere nothings all;
> The world itself, one of ten million bubbles all;
> Lit up by God's own beam, one moment bright;
> 'Tis all I know—the rest is dark as night.[12]

Randall frequently visited the Abbot home. This quiet man took an interest in the three younger children, but he became particularly interested in the sensitive boy with the poetic inclinations. In 1851 and almost every summer thereafter, Frank became Randall's guest for a few weeks at Stow and on innumerable other occasions a visitor to his home. The country vacations were "delightfully Bohemian," Frank said later, but this in no way suggests the personal influence that Randall wielded. A few journal entries from May 1851, when Frank was fourteen, indicate the nature of these experiences. The two would proceed by train to what is now Gleasondale, Massachusetts, and then walk to the Randall estate at Stow. "After supper we talked

---

[11]*Memorials of the Class of 1834 of Harvard College* (Boston, 1884). Quoted in Abbot, "Randall," 48. This memoir by Abbot is the most extensive account of his life. It deals especially with Abbot's personal association and reprints many revealing diary accounts and letters.

[12]The poem is found in [John W. Randall,] *The Consolations of Solitude* (Boston, 1856). Abbot later edited a volume of collected poems, *Poems of Nature and Life* (Boston, 1899), in which these were included.

and read, and, as I was pretty tired, we went to bed early." Forty years later Abbot reminisced: "I shall never forget the brilliant and fascinating way in which during two or three hours, he told me De La Motte Fouque's exquisite story of Undine." Stories and conversation were, of course, major components of Abbot's association with Randall, but by no means were they the only ones. Frank's diaries reveal the long walks, the exciting trips by horse and buggy into the forests and mountains, the swims in mountain brooks, and the constant absorption of nature's lore. Giving a statistical résumé of his first visit to Stow, Frank recorded that his weight had gone up three pounds—to ninety-six and a half, and that they had covered fifty miles on foot, sixty by carriage, and sixty by railroad.[13]

Poetry and philosophy were their most serious concerns. These two pursuits were immediately blended in the studious attention that they gave to Randall's poems. "In his desire to have something written to read to me at our expected Saturday night sessions lay the origin of 'The Consolations of Solitude,' 'The Metamorphoses of Longing,' and other poems." Nor were such poems merely read and forgotten; for weeks on end the two labored to make them acceptable for publication. The first entry in Frank's college diary records the most recent two-week visit to Stow, where they had given another "work-over" to a volume that would be published the following year. The passing years resulted in less-frequent meetings, but they were by no means discontinued. Almost every vacation provided an occasion for a short reunion, and the two men corresponded on a wide range of subjects until Randall's death in 1892.

"I have been preparing this winter to enter the Public Latin School," wrote Frank in July 1851, "and I was to be examined today; so, after breakfast, about nine o'clock, Father went to the school-house with me." It is not hard to imagine the "pale little scholar" walking with his austere father to the school building on Bedford Street. The regulations for entrance required the scholar to be at least ten years old, of good moral character, and competent in certain academic disciplines. After being examined in arithmetic, English grammar, geography, and spelling, Abbot joined what was called the "Fifth Class," the equivalent of a present-day eighth grade. The class was a big one, consisting of nearly one-fourth of the 204 boys enrolled in the school. Frank's class included six boys who would accompany him into the

---

[13]Diary, 3 May 1851; Abbot, "Randall," 74, 84.

Class of 1859 at Harvard. Esprit was high and the boys seemed to stick together at college; but wide-ranging camaraderie was not a feature of these years for Frank. Certainly Frank did not join in fights on the Common with the "Blackguards" from the slums whom Henry Adams described.[14]

The school building was not a lively place; and even though it was relatively new when Abbot entered its halls, one can hardly avoid quoting the reminiscences of George Santayana, who attended thirty years later.

> There is one image above all others that survives from the wreckage of my school days: the picture of the old Bedford Street Schoolhouse. There is no beauty in it, and little of intrinsic interest; but for me it has become a symbol. . . . The Bedford Street Schoolhouse was, or seemed, a vast rickety old shell of a building, bare, shabby, and forlorn to the point of squalor; not dirty exactly, but worn, shaky, and stained deeply in every part by time, weather, and merciless usage. The dingy old brickwall—everything in that world was dingy red brick—had none of those soft pink lights or mossy patina or plastic inequalities of surface which make some old brickwalls so beautiful. They remained stark and unyielding in spite of time, thin and sharp like impoverished old maids; and the glassy expanse of those great rattling window-sashes, cut into many panes, and movable with difficulty, remained blank and vacant.[15]

The building had been erected in 1844 to accommodate the Latin and English schools; as school buildings went, its construction had been thought extravagant. But the passage of time soon revealed its shortcomings. It was not well suited to the uses of the school, and the staircases were lofty, winding, narrow, dark, and dangerous. Moreover, there was almost no playground and Bedford Street was noisy with the continual clatter of horses' hooves and wagons that rendered classroom work almost impossible when the windows were opened.

In those years it was a three-story brick structure with a granite facade. The Latin School occupied two classrooms on each of the two lower floors and a large hall on the third. In this large "hall" the master's platform and desk, on the Bedford Street side, commanded the

---

[14]For an extensive account of the examination, see Diary, 14 July 1851. For town/gown relations, see Henry Adams, *The Education of Henry Adams* (Boston: Houghton, Mifflin, and Co., 1927) 41.

[15]George Santayana, "Glimpses of Old Boston," *Boston Latin School Register* (March 1932).

room. At the end of the room, to the right, stood the declamation platform. It was in this room, every sixth Saturday, that public exhibi-
tions were held for the edification of parents and adult friends who
were interested in hearing the declamations of "those who [had] distinguished themselves at the previous ordinary exercises in this art."
The walls were lined with paintings of classical ruins, a plaster cast of
the shield of Achilles, and portraits of former masters. On brackets or
tables were cork models of the Colosseum and ancient temples, plaster casts of ancient sculptures, and other "curious antiquities."[16]

The curriculum of this venerable institution had not departed
much from the ideals of Ezekiel Cheever, the old worthy of Latin
grammar fame. The Puritanism was less rigid, to be sure, but the classics were entrenched within the program. Charles W. Eliot, who entered the school in 1844, described the school's limitations with a note
of acrimony:

> Sixty-six years ago, when I entered it, the subjects of instruction were
> Latin, Greek, mathematics, English composition and declamation, and
> the elements of Greek and Roman history. There was no formal in-
> struction in the English language and literature, no modern lan-
> guage, no science, and no physical training, or military drill. In short,
> the subjects of instruction were what they had been for two hundred
> years.[17]

Despite Eliot's judgment of this regimen, important values were
inculcated and many former students were less harsh in their evalu-
ations. Phillips Brooks looked back upon it as "the place where were
gathered some of the deepest inspirations that ever came to us." Santayana, too, saw the value of this traditional program, and if he had
little commendation for the building or the administration, he praised
the ideal.

> In spite of all revolutions and all the pressure of business and all the
> powerful influences inclining America to live in contemptuous igno-
> rance of the rest of the world and especially of the past, the Latin
> School . . . has kept the embers of traditional learning alive, at which

---

[16]*Catalogue of the Scholars in the Latin Grammar School in Boston* (1852)
16-17; Henry Fitch Jenks, *Catalogue of the Boston Public Latin School*
(Boston, 1886) 96. See also his *The Boston Public Latin School, 1835-1880*
(Cambridge MA, 1881).

[17]Eliot quoted in Pauline Holmes, *A Tercentenary History of the Boston
Public Latin School* [Harvard Studies in Education, No. 25] (Cambridge:
Harvard University Press, 1935) 275.

the humblest rush-light might always be lighted. . . . This fidelity to tradition, I am confident, had and will have its reward. The oldest forms of life, barring accidents, have the longest future. New ideas in their violence and new deeds in their urgency pass like a storm; and then the old earth, seared and enriched by those trials, finds itself still under the same sky, unscarred and pure as before.[18]

Though never so ardent a champion of the classical tradition as Santayana, Abbot frequently repeated this assessment of his schooling and gave thanks for the foundations that it had provided.

The man who, during these years, supervised this process of educating Boston's "better" boys was Francis Gardner. One of Gardner's pupils later commented that "whatever else he lacked, [this great master] had character, not of the finelined, sentimental kind, cut and polished as a well proportioned statue, but in bulk, a massive bulwark protesting against all cant, superciliousness, and untruth." The accuracy of this general picture of Francis Gardner is underlined by the report of a citizen's committee that charged him for being rude in speech, ungentlemanly in his admonitions, and "actuated more by a desire to gratify anger than to secure reform, in administering punishments." Nonetheless, nobody ever questioned his knowledge of the classical languages, especially Latin, and his ability by rough means or soft to pass on his learning to his pupils.[19]

Such then was the scene: an uninspiring building, a forbidding headmaster, and an inflexible, unimaginative curriculum. As a scholar confronting this environment, however, Abbot was a success from the very beginning. During his first year at the school, Abbot was cited for "exemplary conduct and punctuality" and awarded the prize for English poetry. In the following year he showed the same excellent behavior and was also cited for excellence in both the Classical and Modern Departments. Abbot also won the prize for English poetry a second time. During his last year at the school, 1853-1854, he was cited for good behavior, for excellence in both departments, for the best Latin poem, and for his translation from Sallust. His stay in Boston ended in 1854 when his brother Edwin, then a senior at Harvard, offered to tutor him for a year.

---

[18]Brooks is quoted in Jenks, *Catalogue,* 121; Santayana in "The Boston Latin School," in a program for the Tercentenary Exercises, 23 April 1935.

[19]Jenks, *Catalogue,* 55; *Report of the Committee of the Latin School on the Remonstrance of Thirty Four Persons against the Re-election of Francis Gardner, Esq. as Master of Said School* (Boston, 26 April 1865).

Yet the question of what a diligent, brilliant boy had received when he completed his Latin School education remains. One can be certain only as to the question of what and how much he learned. On this we have both the records and his word. He was a stellar pupil while attending the Boston Latin School and he achieved the second-highest mark for his year's Harvard entrance exam. Abbot often remarked that the thorough training in Latin that he received made it almost unnecessary for him to study the language at Harvard. Three decades later he looked over the education scene and concluded that "no school teaches half as well as I was taught at Boston Latin School."

On a deeper level, however, any adequate consideration would involve describing the confident, optimistic, and yet moralistic outlook of antebellum Boston. It is clear the school was chiefly concerned with preparing students for further classical studies in college. The core of the curriculum centered around fundamental academic and literary skills. Although religion received little formal emphasis, nothing was done that did not support the essential doctrines of liberal Christianity, which characterized much of the city's Protestantism. Adam's sin was no longer inexorably associated with the first letter of the alphabet. The truths of natural religion, the ethics of Jesus, and the certainty of an eternal reward for a somewhat legalistically conceived righteousness were assumed. If the boy evidenced a more evangelical outlook, it was due to the influence of his parents or church, for the classical emphasis of the school tended rather to modify and secularize such a point of view.

The impact of this classical tradition must be specially reckoned with even though it was almost lost under the debris of syntax and grammar. Even George Santayana, who is certainly not known for his Boston enthusiasms, recognized the force and value of the "directive mission" of the Boston Latin School. For the serious-minded student whose background in the classical languages had been thorough, there can be no doubt that the moral earnestness and social consciousness of Livy, Sallust, Virgil, and Seneca left their mark.

CHAPTER TWO

HARVARD

ON 17 JULY 1855 the gathering of prospective Harvard students for the Class of 1859 took place in room 16 of University Hall—and they were quite a varied lot. There were the well-schooled sons of wealthy parents, rivaling Francis French of the Class of 1857. Francis had a well-stocked wine cellar, a manservant, and a team of horses at his disposal. Others were poverty-stricken objects of charity, such as C. A. Daniels, Abbot's classmate, who was in college due to the interest of a local minister and the generosity of a merchant. Daniels started to board out at $3.00 a week, but when this proved too expensive he "lived on soda crackers and water with an occasional piece of cheese for a relish, at a cost of less than a dollar a week." Indeed the Boston Latin School boys coming out from Boston on the omnibus were themselves of widely different stations and means.

The material upon which these aspirants were to be examined could hardly be regarded as trivial. The classics department laid down requirements for the whole of Virgil and Caesar, selected orations of Cicero, focused on Latin grammar including prosody, and required the ability to write the language correctly. In Greek the examiners asked for a knowledge of Felton's *Reader,* Sophocles' *Grammar,* and the ability to write Greek with the accents. The math department required a grounding in algebra and geometry. The history department reflected its status in the university by insisting only upon a knowledge of Mitchell's *Ancient and Modern Geography,* and the ancient-history sections of Worcester's *Elements of History.* Abbot had little difficulty with these subjects and was ranked the highest in his class.[1]

These were halcyon days in Cambridge. Harvard Square, still shaded by a fine old elm, was referred to as "the Village"; not more than a dozen places of business were situated there, and the public hay scales to which surrounding farmers brought their loads for

---

[1]Examination areas noted in Harvard *Catalogue,* Second Term, 1854-1855. Abbot's experiences are recounted in Diary, 27 September 1855.

weighing were still a prominent feature.[2] The Harvard railroad branch had ceased to operate in 1855 and only the four-horse omnibuses, running every half-hour, plied between the Square and the West Boston bridge. The two-horse omnibuses operating out from the Square were used to supplement the regular service. It was a beautiful and frequently taken walk out to Mount Auburn; Fresh Pond was in the country; and Norton's Woods stretched out in back of the Yard to the northeast. In recollection, Francis G. Peabody concluded, with possibly more sentiment than accuracy, that the faculty mirrored this situation.

> These neighbors did not seem to be of the large world, nor was their conversation concerned with the events and problems of their age. On the contrary they seemed singularly segregated and limited in interest, and had almost the qualities of a monastic order, . . . Yet if this segregation meant simplicity and unworldliness, it meant also elevation of mind and felicity of thought. What they cared for was worth caring, and their talk was not of money or gossip, but of ideas and neighborly amenities. . . . Their world was small, but it was high up and the air was pure. . . . It was the secluded life of a village community, but it was fraternal and genuine.[3]

The college Yard and buildings offered a rather imposing prospect. Indeed, one of the professors who had been impressed by the Göttingen library suggested that Harvard had placed entirely too much confidence in brick and stone. All the college buildings, except Divinity Hall, were in the Yard: Holworthy across the north side of the old quadrangle, Stoughton, Hollis, Harvard, Massachusetts, and Dane extended down the east side, with Holden Chapel still farther west between Hollis and Stoughton. Wadsworth House, which had been the presidential mansion down through Edward Everett's term as president, was at the south on what is now Massachusetts Avenue. On the west side of the quadrangle was University Hall, then facing only to the east and housing the chapel, president's office, and classrooms. The only structure beyond this quadrangle was Gore Hall, the

---

[2]Charles W. Eliot, *Harvard Memories* (Cambridge: Harvard University Press, 1923) 95.

[3]Francis G. Peabody, *Harvard in the Sixties: A Boy's Eye View* (Cambridge, 1935) 19-20. See also Andrew Preston Peabody, *Harvard Reminiscences* (Boston, 1888); and Charles J. White, ed., "Diary of a Classmate," *Records of the Class of 1859* (Boston, 1896), hereafter referred to as "Anonymous Diary."

library. In 1858, however, Boylston Hall was completed in the southeast corner of the old quad, and used for chemistry, mineralogy, and a related "collection." The same year saw the completion of Appleton Chapel, and two years later an octagonal gymnasium was erected on the lesser Delta where the fire station now stands. This was the physical plant—and for a student body of fewer than five hundred undergraduates it could hardly have been called inadequate.[4]

Abbot's financial worries as he entered Harvard were considerable, but his earnestness made up for the deficit. "[I] would make ten times the sacrifice rather than forego my education." He promised himself to study hard; and with the systematic approach that was to characterize all of his life's endeavors, he supplied the reasons in his opening confidences to his diary: to make his debt worthwhile, to please his parents, and to increase his chances for a scholarship and later a job. Moreover, Frank admitted, "I have vanity enough to be pleased with the idea of excelling."

A desire for moral growth led him to initiate a journal that he would continue for the rest of his life: "My object is self-improvement; and I think one means to this end will be the faithful transcript of my sorrows and joys." It is accurate to say that Abbot's fears and sorrows overbalanced his hopes and joys. The first stirrings of his young romantic heart, along with a moral Punch and Judy show between his conscience and a passion for tobacco filled his diary with remorse and self-recrimination. Although these problems may seem quaint to the modern reader, they played havoc with the sensitive young college student. Yet more basic than any of these difficulties was Frank's eternal *douleur,* a loneliness that led him into a continuous search for close companionship. Eventually he would be rewarded in the friendship of a calm, earnest classmate, William Reed Huntington, who would become a famous Episcopal cleric. Abbot and Huntington were drawn together by a mutual appreciation for the poetry of William Cullen Bryant. To the young Abbot, such a friendship was a pure godsend: "When we started together, I grew more calm, and showed no evidence of the whirlwind of emotion which had filled my breast; I could not resist the sweet belief that he loved me, and as I yielded to it, I felt a happiness which has never been my lot before."[5]

---

[4]Samuel Eliot Morison, *Three Centuries of Harvard* (Cambridge: Harvard University Press, 1936) passim.

[5]Diary, 26 November 1856.

Despite a troubled spirit and a precarious financial situation, there is nothing to indicate that Abbot was forced into a cramped social life. The unity of a Harvard class was an extreme thing in those years; and the loyalty first established in the "football game" between freshmen and sophomores persisted until the last members of the class had died. They made up a convivial group and Frank's journal is replete with references to their interactions. Yet levity did not always provide the keynote. "I went into Swan's room, read our customary chapter of the Bible, and then I came back and here I am writing," he wrote one November evening. On other occasions Abbot and other students would get together for private readings of Catullus.

Abbot was exceedingly diligent in his course work; but aside from his regular studies, the Anonyma, a society for freshmen, provided him with excellent opportunities to accommodate both his social and scholarly instincts. It was, as the invitation to membership tersely declared, "a strictly secret society." Each fall the retiring sophomores selected a group of the fifteen most promising freshmen to carry on the "tradition" of the club, which dated back to the school year of 1853-1854. Before the end of September Frank received his invitation, which also contained a list of the other new members. Shortly afterward he went to the first meeting to elect officers and choose thirty more freshmen. An elaborate initiation ceremony came next. After the ceremony the group traveled by omnibus to the Fresh Pond Hotel where the departing sophomores were feted. It was a night of good food, great quantities of wine and champagne, speeches, songs, and ribaldry. Frank abstained from everything save a cigar and tersely ended his account of the drunken busride back: "Haydon broke a bottle over Bradford's head, and vomited all over Cutting. We got home about one o'clock."[6] This somewhat bacchanalian opening, however, did not characterize the year's activities. The weekly meetings were serious, consisting usually of debates on various philosophical or historical subjects.

Abbot's college life continued along these general lines through the fall term of 1856. With winter vacation of 1856-1857 coming, Frank had to face the prospect of teaching for fifteen weeks in order to supplement his income. Being excused from part of the term, he took a position as acting principal of an academy in Concord, and acceptance of this post made him responsible for classes in Latin, Greek, geometry, Shakespeare, Plutarch, composition, and declamation. But it was

---

[6]Ibid., 27 September; 3, 4, and 7 October 1855.

not just the teaching experience that made these months in Concord memorable for him. It was here that Frank met the girl (she was seventeen then) who was to be his love in all the years that followed. Among the last words he ever wrote was the dedication for his final work (*The Syllogistic Philosophy*):

TO THE MEMORY

of

MY WIFE

*In Whose Divine Beauty of Character, Life
and Soul
I Found the God I Sought*

It was apotheosis: her love was the love of God. Yet she entered his life simply enough.

> I went to a party at Mrs. Dana's ten days ago, and was introduced to Miss Kate Loring, a most charming and lovely girl; she seemed to feel so much compassion for me, alone and sick, among perfect strangers, that I was really very much touched by it. I danced with her twice or three times, and found her very pleasant and well-informed, and very lady-like. I thought of her all night instead of going to sleep. If there ever was a fool, his name is Frank Abbot.[7]

A year later she confided her recollections of the event to him.

> Henry Dalton came up and asked me if I would be introduced to you. I said "No" at first, but afterward I said "Yes"; and at the same time determined to make you pay more attention to me than you did to anyone else, merely because I liked to receive attention, but I had not talked with you ten minutes before I forgot all about that and really wanted you to like me.[8]

Katharine Fearing Loring was the daughter of David Loring, who had been one of Concord's more successful entrepreneurs. He was a strong, short man, swarthy and handsome, self-made and self-educated. Loring was also known as a hard, honest businessman, taciturn but strong in his convictions, devoted in religion and a conservative Whig politically. Shortly after the Loring family had moved into the fine old Josiah Davis estate, Katharine was born on 18 October 1839. Her fragile health made it seem unlikely that she would reach adulthood. In fact, she was very slightly built and never strong, but she was

---

[7]Ibid., 17 January 1857.
[8]Katie to FEA, 11 January 1858.

also quiet, gentle, and beautiful. In later years Katharine had been well enough to attend school, and her father spoke of her proudly as a "cultivated young lady."

Circumstance cooperated with their romance. The town was caught that season in a series of snowstorms that confined nearly everyone, and Katie dropped a flatiron on her foot so that she was further restricted. The poetry of Bryant again provided the initial interest and was followed by selections from the whole sweep of British and American letters. From this point Katharine and Frank moved to John Randall's verse, then to Frank's, and finally to the imagery of mutual love. Scarcely three weeks later Frank took a walk with Mr. Loring and gained his consent for Katie's hand, although her parents would not allow a public announcement of their engagement until 1 May.

A week after Frank and Katharine became informally engaged, the Lorings left Concord for Crawfordsville, Indiana. Frank was lonely, but it was a new kind of loneliness; for he saw quite clearly that an important transition had been accomplished. Frank regaled his correspondents again with the news, and received their congratulations in return. Perhaps nothing proves the salutary effect of his romance so much as the fact that upon his return to Harvard an entire month passed before Frank so much as made an entry in his diary. Frank admitted, "It takes my self-control more than a little to check the despondency which will spring up in my solitary hours, sided as it is by my constitutional melancholy," but he seems to have gained the solace that he had sought so desperately. The importance of the Huntington friendship is clear. "Had I not vanquished my old enemy before going to Concord, I doubt much if I could have fallen in love with Katie," he wrote at the end of his sophomore year. No one could doubt that it was Katie who enabled him to say (possibly for the first time in his life), "I am now *happy*, yes, *happy*, in spite of debt and uncheerful prospects."[9]

Frank later admitted, when he commenced keeping his journal again, that his "inner life has not been connected much with the everyday incidents through which I have passed. My dreams have all been of Katie." Yet some recapitulation of "everyday incidents" might be of value, even though it involves picking up strands that precede his romantic revolution.

The extracurricular activities that occupied him most were the weekly meetings of the Institute of 1770. This was a society with the

---

[9]FEA to Katie, 10 March 1857; Diary, 12 July 1857.

same purposes as the Anonyma though it was mellowed by an older tradition. Its exercises were purely literary, with each weekly meeting consisting of a fifteen-minute lecture, a debate, a paper edited by four members, and a critique of the preceding meeting by an "unknown hand."[10] The lectures were usually more philosophical and less timely than the debates, while the editorials were often on college problems. "Promiscuous discussion," according to the minutes, followed most of the events of these meetings. Abbot was one of the four editors of the paper until his departure for teaching compelled his resignation. The editorials of his that have been preserved reveal a vigorous opponent of horseplay, profanity, and undue noise. Even his occasional humor takes a satirical or indignant tone.

During the last days of April 1857, the Lorings returned to Concord and moved into a cottage in town; they lived there until June, when they moved to Framingham. Katie's proximity made the final months of school more pleasant for Frank. He visited her in Concord and Katie came to Beverly during Frank's spring vacation. Even if he was happier than he had ever been before, Frank's melancholy reasserted itself. "My God! I could not live without her, and drag on through weary, weary years," he wrote in April. His anxiety was echoed, strangely, by Katie. "When you are away from me I have a feeling of fear. I can not tell what it is that I fear but the feeling is strong enough to make me unhappy sometimes." Frank answered, "I have the same."[11]

The faculty proclaimed a holiday for Edward Everett's Cambridge oration on 18 June. Abbot used the occasion to combine that holiday with Class Day and a weekend in order to spend four days in Framingham with Katie. It was during this time that Katie returned her engagement ring. Frank could say little when she gave her reasons: "Just before I left Crawfordsville, the very night before I came away, I heard a voice tell me not 'to love you so much.' . . . God meant that I should love him first, and you next; but I find I am loving you first." Frank took the ring and wore it over his heart with a lock of her hair until Katie agreed to wear it again. Returning to school he was involved in the final round of events.

---

[10]For an account of the meetings, see *Catalogue of the Officers and Members of the Institute of 1770 of Harvard University* (Cambridge, 1857) iii; and Francis O. French, *Exeter and Harvard Eighty Years Ago* (Chester NH: Privately printed, 1932) 73.

[11]Diary, 29 April 1857; Katie to FEA, 5 June 1857; FEA to Katie, 7 June 1857.

I am in the midst of the terrible "Examinations." Wednesday I was examined in Mathematics, and I rejoice to say that hereafter I am forever freed from them as studies; today, in Greek and Chemistry. One of the committee told another student (a freshman) that I "did most splendidly [in Greek]." What do you think of that? I also came off quite well in Chemistry, though I did not take the committee quite off their seats by the resplendent glories of my recitation. Tomorrow I shall be examined in Latin and then—hooray for vacation!!!![12]

In September 1857, after a summer of indolence and visiting, Frank began his third year in Hollis Hall. A decision to take on a private pupil in Latin and Greek brought on the main revision of his college routine. Tutoring would bring him a hundred dollars and be less arduous than keeping school during winter vacation. Yet Frank's third year at Harvard would be remembered for far more than his freedom from keeping school, because it marked an important transition in his life.

"I hardly know why, but my heart is sick within me; everything is black," he wrote to Katie in early October. The remark presaged another spiritual crisis, which, however absurd it may seem, was the most painful that Abbot experienced in his college career. For one with his immensely proud nature, it was what he said it was, "a fiery ordeal." Katie got the story in a letter.

Last night there was a meeting of our Society. . . . After the exercises were through, and before the motion to adjourn was made, I got up and spoke these words, as nearly as I can recollect them:—

"Gentlemen, I wish to ask your attention for a few moments to a communication of a wholly private nature. I wish to make a statement of facts which must produce a change in your opinion of me, and that for the worse. Nearly five years ago I foolishly began to wear eyeglasses, without being nearsighted. From that time to this I have been acting a continual falsehood, because I had not the moral courage to throw off the cheat. I have tried to find some way of easing my conscience and sparing my pride at the same time, such as feigning a gradual recovery, or taking some other contemptible half-way course. But it was of no use. The only manly course left me was open confession. Accordingly I here publicly declare myself to have been for nearly five years a systematic deceiver."[13]

---

[12]Diary, 21 June 1857; FEA to Katie, 9 July 1857.

[13]FEA to Katie, 6 October 1857.

Abbot went on for two more pages, still quoting his speech, telling how he would surely lose friends and shock all who knew him, but he would still bear the awful ignominy. To Katie he explained the origins of his habit, tracing it to a boyish vanity that he never had the strength to disavow even though he came to see "this one trifling sin . . . [as] a barrier betwixt me and God." He then absolved her from their engagement.

Modern readers may smile, but just as in the case of St. Augustine's pears, the religious significance of this "ordeal" was major. The "mortification" that accompanied it marks a turning point in Abbot's attitude towards his own sinfulness. Katie had long pointed the way that he now began to follow: "Do not say that if I can not give you 'comfort and encouragement' you do not know where to look for it. Dear Frank, there is One who will give you comfort and strength to bear your troubles if you only ask Him."[14] From the earliest times his mother had counseled him likewise: "I *know* you can become a Christian," she would say whenever he brought his tribulations to her, "not alone, but with divine help." On the night of 5 November came Frank's annual moral inspection as the clock tolled out the last day of his boyhood. "I feel as far (if not more far) from God as before," he said; but before this he had hardly been measuring the relation.[15]

In youth Abbot had been geared to the conservative Unitarianism of the Reverend Ephraim Peabody, whose words and life were so dear to his mother. As a freshman in college Frank admitted that his early "childlike faith" had been undermined by the skeptical rationalism of John Randall. All that remained, substantially, was moral earnestness and the crushing sense of responsibility handed down by his father and accentuated no less by family conflicts than by the harsh recommendations of his oldest brother, Henry. Abbot's other brother Edwin was comforted by the teachings of Emanuel Swedenborg, yet for Frank the New Church doctrines had only a passing appeal. After reading Theophilus Parsons' *Essays,* Abbot didn't know how much to believe: "I feel interested in Swedenborgianism," he wrote as a freshman, "and I think many of the doctrines are very beautiful, but I have not read enough to form a decided opinion. May God Almighty enlighten me that I may see the truth."[16] The moderate liberalism of

---

[14]Katie to FEA, 8 October 1857.

[15]Mother to FEA, 23 January 1857; Diary, 5-6 November 1857.

[16]Diary, 16 December 1855. Parsons (1797-1882) was an enthusiastic lay advocate of Swedenborg. Abbot was probably reading the first series of *Essays,* published in 1845. Edwin also sent Frank a copy of Swedenborg's *Heaven and Hell.* Edwin Hale Abbot to FEA, 1 February 1857.

Charles Kingsley's diverse writings seemed to be most satisfying and Bryant was Abbot's spiritual lodestar. When he was thirteen his mother's reading of "Thanatopsis" had done much to awaken his interest in poetry. Bryant's poems also had been central in the "discovery" of William Huntington and in his courtship of Katie. That a veritable "passion" for Bryant and his work should become Frank Abbot's deepest intellectual commitment, therefore, is hardly surprising.

The poet's evocation of nature's primordial lessons had a peculiar meaning for a lonely boy wandering in the Wilton countryside, and at the same time they guided him to a closer communion with "Nature's God." The opening lines of "Thanatopsis," or these lines from "A Forest Hymn" must have seemed like gospel:

> But let me often to these solitudes
> Retire, and in thy presence reassure
> My feeble virtue. Here its enemies,
> The passions, at thy plainer footsteps shrink
> And tremble and are still . . .

As to the brooding concern for death that is so basic to Bryant, its appeal is easy to explain in one with Frank's early insecurities and fragile health. Nor was it a superficial poetic pose: there is good reason for believing that this was the main basis of Frank's attraction to Bryant. Abbot was haunted by death; a mournful preoccupation with its problems marks almost all of his youthful poems. The same agonizing note pervades even his warmest letters to Katie. Finally, it was probably Abbot's readiness for Bryant's philosophic outlook that was of decisive significance. Bryant was a Unitarian and his religious philosophy was tempered by a classical rationalism, bound to a deep regard for Greek and Roman literature. Bryant was not a "man of feeling" and he would never become a follower of the Transcendentalists. His was a stoical recognition of human temporality moderated by an optimistic faith in human progress. To the troubled and thoughtful Harvard student it had been an adequate, reasonable answer. Whether coincidence, effect, or cause (or partly each) it is impossible to tell, but the storm of self-criticism that preceded and followed the public confession was accompanied by a gradual reorientation of mind. The forces that brought Abbot to this juncture are various and widely separated.

The simplest to locate is the great national revival of 1857-1858 that was rolling over the country. "I do not approve of these 'revivals,' " he said, but their influence was undeniable. They even infiltrated the Harvard Yard, where the university preacher openly espoused the cause. Second, the cumulative effect of many friends, from William Huntington and George Chaney (a Harvard classmate) to his mother and brother Edwin, was very important. Almost as direct was the influence of various faculty members such as Josiah Parsons Cooke, professor of chemistry, who sponsored small, informal religious meetings every Sunday evening; Professor Frederic Dan Huntington, who brought to his duties as Plummer Professor and university preacher the evangelical fervor that was to carry him on into the Episcopal Church; and President Walker, whose great sermons, reflecting the old Unitarian tradition of piety, brought new emphasis to the religion of the heart.

The real problem that Frank faced, however, was personal and internal. His fundamental melancholy remained, but it encountered new circumstances now. His great love for Katie was the difference. As life became freighted with so much love, it seemed to become more precarious. The loss that loomed inexorably in the future seemed now to be infinite. He set out upon a search, and the letters to Katie reveal the pilgrim's progress.

> I will try to pray oftener hereafter, dear Katie, I have been thinking of Christ's religion a great deal lately, and I feel a very strong desire to lead a pure and blameless life, one that shall be devoted to working in his cause. I think it more than probable I shall join the college church soon. It is so constituted as to include all who have the deep desire of holiness, irrespective of any sectarian belief. *I think that I have come to the grand crisis of my life, when I must make my final decision whether I will yield myself up to God's will, or whether I will still live as I have done, without a settled principle of action.* The struggle is a very violent one, but I hope the result will be a great victory. But I am assailed with doubts and temptations, and at times I am almost determined to give up the contest. Pray for me now if you ever prayed for me, and if you wish our future life to be knit with the only bonds that can make it firmly and indissolubly one. I shall feel a deeper sorrow than I have ever yet felt, if I do not find you growing an earnest and trusting Christian. It is dreadful for a man to be irreligious; for a woman, it is inexpressibly bad. Darling, let us be bound together in the love of Christ, and become his humble disciples.[17]

To Katie he also became, as it were, a sort of missionary to the missioner.

---

[17]FEA to Katie, 14 March 1858.

How I hope you will sympathize in my wish to lead a pure and up-right life. . . . I never wished anything more deeply than I now wish you to become a sincere, practical Christian; not a merely nominal one, but one who feels that religion only gives its value to life. I know you are much nearer to such Christianity than I; but I hope you will think about it and make up your mind *deliberately* to serve that tender Shepherd who would fain gather us all into his fold. I have made my choice; I mean honestly to try to be a Christian, and if I am sure it will keep me in this object, I shall join the college chapel. I do not ap-prove these "revivals," which make religion a matter of impulse and excitement; they are very apt to be followed by a reaction. But it is right to come forward calmly, and state our serious intention to live according to Christ's dictates, if so doing will strengthen us in carry-ing out this intention. At any rate, our lives must show on which side we mean to take our stand in the battle of life. I shall probably take this step of becoming a member of the church, if mother thinks it a wise one. I could not join any church but this, because it is peculiarly constituted. It includes all who wish to live Christian lives, irrespec-tive of all creeds or sectarian beliefs. I could not subscribe any creed, at least at present; my faith is too little settled. But to partake of the Lord's Supper will be a great help, and I wish to avail myself of it. Pray God the time may come when we shall partake of it together. Write to me freely just what you think of my taking this step, and how you feel yourself in regard to such matters.

Katie, in response, indicated her pleasure that he had joined the church, saying that she wished to do the same. "I truly wish to be one of Christ's lambs," she declared. Three days later, doubting that her desire to show herself as "one of Christ's followers will ever cool off," Frank urged her to delay until he could be present for "this most im-portant step." On his own account, though, Frank acted immediately.

I went to Dr. Huntington's and signed the paper which makes me a member of his church. I should not have done it if I had not had some objections which prevented me wholly removed by some explana-tions made by Prof. Cooke to Ned Curtis. These convinced me that I could conscientiously sign the paper, which I therefore did. So that now I am in truth one of Christ's open disciples. May he help me walk on bravely in the path I have chosen. I am *so* glad that you will be my companion.

On the following Sunday the transition was solemnized.

Katie, I joined the little band of believers around the Lord's table, for the first time, this morning. I hope and pray it may help me in living according to Jesus' teachings. Our future home will be all the happier that we strive to make it a Christian one. It would have been a delightful thought to me to think that you had been the cause of such great good to me.[18]

Abbot's correspondence provides a key insight into Unitarian piety at mid-century, which was neither classically evangelical (since it did not culminate in a conversion experience) nor comfortably latitudinarian; instead, it followed a different mode. Abbot's "conversion" was a willingness to commit himself to a view of life. Frank's advice to Katie, "Our lives must show on which side we mean to take our stand in the battle of life," became a standard for the rest of his life.

Just when Frank decided to take the further step of entering upon a pastoral career is not perfectly clear. Abbot intimated he was thinking of it in June 1858, and by the end of the schoolyear his plans were at least of a deeply religious cast.

> Oh Katie, I want to see you regard life as I regard it, a vineyard where we can do our Master service. . . . Faith can look through the clouds and see the brightness of the glory beyond—let us take her into our hearts and learn of Jesus. Then the hour of parting, which *must* come, will lose its sting, and all will be closer in the blessed light of God.[19]

Yet even before this Abbot had turned his organizational abilities to religious purposes by becoming the founding spirit of the Christian Union. This society began with an informal meeting on the evening of 18 October 1857 when a group of students assembled "to consider the expediency of forming a new Religious Society in the College." Abbot was behind this move, and the constitution came from his hand, stating the club's objectives as follows: "to secure the moral and religious improvement of the members;—to elevate the standard of morality in College, and to spread among us Christian sentiments, unsectarian and liberal." Abbot was elected president for the first term, with George Chaney serving the second term. The weekly meetings consisted of Scripture reading and prayer by the president, the reading of a sermon or appropriate devotion by a member or visiting speaker, a hymn, and a closing prayer.

Abbot's other extracurricular activities during his junior year were not extensive. Scholastic ambition, tutoring a pupil, romantic diversions, and a three-week interruption for the removal of a varicose vein from his throat would have prevented other commitments even if Frank's pocketbook had not. As it was, Abbot even lacked money for

---

[18]Ibid., (c.) 20, 28 March; 4 April 1858.

[19]Ibid., 11 July 1858.

postage to send Katie a birthday present—a book into which he had copied a hundred pages of his own poetry.

On 20 September 1858, after summer vacation, Frank was back in Cambridge. He and William Huntington decided to take a class in the Sunday school that Professor Huntington conducted in his home on Sunday afternoons. Frank was assigned to a group of girls, many of them professors' daughters. The fall term was not especially eventful. He took part in the Exhibition Day ceremonies during October, studied hard, and saw Katie as much as possible.

The winter vacation he spent at home and in good spirits. Frank tutored his sister Emily in geometry, French, and other subjects. He studied his own work, nursed a cold, and warded off the nostrums that his father proposed. In March, while his true love wrote of mockingbirds and orange blossoms, Frank went back to Cambridge for an all-out attack on his academic duties.

Finally, on 24 June 1859 came Class Day. "It began to drizzle about 6 a.m. and drizzled more or less during the day till $5\frac{1}{2}$, when it stopped." Nevertheless, the academic procession, headed by the "Germania Band," proceeded to First Parish meetinghouse. The Cambridge *Courier* observed that the "inevitable last man in line" was duly berated and that as usual the college faculty never kept step with the music. The ceremony began at 11:00 "precisely," despite the impossibly large throng that attempted to gain entrance. The *Advertiser* testified that the audience that filled the building was an "attentive and brilliant" one. The program followed the traditional pattern:

Music by the Band
A prayer by the Rev. Dr. Walker
The Class Oration by Francis V. Balch
Music
The Class Poem by William Reed Huntington
The singing of the Class Ode [written by Francis E. Abbot]

The press was indulgent in review: "It would be manifestly improper as well as contrary to custom, to subject the performances to a rigid analysis or criticism; it is sufficient to say that they were characterized by sound sense and good taste, and showed that the culture of Cambridge maintains its high standard." President Walker's prayer received no comment, but it was said that "there were some bright gleams of wit" in the poem, "which refreshed all, and startled into laughter even the parietal gravity of the Proctors." To modern readers the poem seems rather dull, but the Anonymous Diary said it was "full of fun and pun and joke." The oration was a well-worded, though ornate, review of "the metamorphic period" during which they had been classmates. The program was concluded by the singing of Abbot's melancholy ode.

I

Once again has the earth lightly whirled round the sun
 In the jubilant dance of the spheres:
Ever youthful, another bright gem she has won,
 To flash in her circlet of years.
But our spring-tide is ebbing, our morning is o'er;
 The moment of parting draws nigh,
And our Mother—God bless her!—stands here at the door
 To throw us a kiss and good-bye.

II

Like the arches and spires that with marble of frost
 The Winter-elf builds on the pane,
Hope's castles may melt and in tear-drops be lost,
 Ere our sun its proud zenith shall gain.
But friendship has rung a sweet chime from her bells,
 Whose echoes, when youth shall decay
Like the music that lurks in the sighing sea-shells,
 Will haunt us and cheer us for aye.

III

As the rain-drops that wed on the river's gray breast
 Are divorced in the broad heaving main,
From the north and the south and the east and the west
 We have met but to scatter again.
The noble old elm waits our time-honored song,
 Let us join "hand to hand, heart to heart";
We have laughed and been merry together full long,
 But the summons is come, and we part.

IV

Yet the friendships of youth, like the Pleiads that weave
 Their soft meshes of splendor on high,
O'er our paths a bright glory of starlight will leave,
 And smile all the gloom from our sky;
Oh cleave to the love that has hallowed the past,—
 It shall hallow the future's long years!
For today, ere life blows her stern clarion blast,
 We baptize it immortal with tears.

Of course there was no dancing on the green in the afternoon, and "the workmen took away the useless music-stand from the center of the nicely shaven lawn, where it had been standing in the pitiless rain all day."[20]

At 5:30 they gathered around the "Rebellion Tree," the old elm that stood between Holden Chapel and Harvard Hall. There they sang "Auld Lang Syne" with all the variations. The garlands were torn from the tree and distributed, and the more violent "running" began. The seniors formed a circle on the inside around the tree; other students joined the outer line, and then they revolved in opposite directions "till catastrophe comes." Afterwards they cheered the buildings first and, though the regulations forbade it, perhaps the professors. In the evening came the Levee, which "featured the fastest waltzing this side of Paris," and between 10:00 and 11:00 the Glee Club sang in the Yard. By midnight the scene was probably reasonably quiet, though two members of the class were given public admonitions (sixty-four-point deductions) for "having a spree" or attending same.[21]

Between Class Day and graduation Frank was busy seeking a teaching position or polishing the periods of his commencement part, which was an affirmation of his convictions about the Christian ministry based on the life of John Horne Tooke, whom he reprimanded

> . . . as a man who spent his wealth of intellect on buying for himself a monopoly of admiration, who cared little for the opinions he advocated save as a tight-rope on which to display his wonderful mental callisthenics. [Most disgraceful of all] He was a minister of the gospel, *and was thoroughly ashamed of his calling,* which he early abandoned for political life. He was eager to show that he could at least be a layman in private licentiousness. . . . If self-glorification is indeed the great god Juggernaut . . . , then the character of Horne Tooke is a notable example for the imitation of all educated men.[22]

When commencement came, on 20 July, Katie was present in the meetinghouse of First Parish for the exercises that began at 11:00 and lasted through forty-one numbers and the awarding of honorary degrees until 2:30 in the afternoon. Thereupon all graduates repaired to the library where they formed a procession by class with the venerable Josiah Quincy in the lead and marched to Harvard Hall for dinner. After dinner Mr. Sibley, the librarian, led them in singing the

---

[20]This account is based on the reports of both the *Daily Advertiser* and the *Courier.*

[21]Anonymous Diary, 28 June 1859.

[22]From MS in Harvard Archives.

78th Psalm. Frank's diary contains only a terse message: "Commencement Day—and the death of my college life."

On the following day came the "annual celebration of the Phi Beta Kappa Society," with a procession of members to First Parish meetinghouse again. Here the Reverend Barnas Sears, president of Brown University, delivered a vigorous defense of classical studies that at least did not prevent Professor Felton from being reelected president of the chapter at the afternoon business meeting. After this day the college festivities were over: Frank now faced "the roar of the great world beyond."[23]

_____

[23]FEA to Katie, 14 April 1859.

CHAPTER THREE

THE MINISTERIAL CANDIDATE

THE PROBLEMS FACED by the new graduate were not simple, though his purpose was clear. "You must fit as earnest to be a minister's wife, as I to be a minister," Frank had written to Katie. "We must work side by side in our Lord's vineyard, and then side by side we shall appear at his Throne and kneel in humble trustfulness for his approving smile." But with debts, family obligations, and three years of divinity school to finance, Abbot could not think of marrying before 1864. By the time of commencement, Frank had revised this to 1862 or 1863. For the present he exploited every possible avenue and influence to get a teaching position. However, since Frank also wanted a Boston location and a high salary, no positions could be found.

The arrival of Katie served to set these frustrations aside, and after a few weeks in Beverly, the two of them accepted a long-standing invitation to visit his relatives in Wilton. Considering all the reverent references to the days they spent in the country, it must have been an idyllic experience. Nor is it strange that they looked fondly on that vacation, for on 3 August 1859, after accepting a farewell blessing from Frank's grandmother, they went down to Nashua, New Hampshire. In Nashua, with all of the participants sworn to secrecy, Frank Abbot and Katie Loring were married by the Reverend Austin Richards of the Olive Street Congregational Church.[1]

The reasons for this decision are fairly clear. Mr. Loring had decided to move his family out to the new state of Minnesota. In Winona, then a busy river town, Katie's father was entering a grocery partnership. Katie and Frank were both convinced that they would be happier in their separation if they were married.

What they did during the months of August and September is not clear. Presumably this time was spent in the usual round of visiting. Since the marriage was an exceedingly well-kept secret, there was assuredly no honeymoon. But on 5 October Katie conveyed to him the calamitous news that she was pregnant.

---

[1]FEA to Richards, 3 August 1859. See also FEA to Katie, 5 May 1860.

The prospect of fatherhood lent a new seriousness to Abbot's predicament and made it more obvious than ever that teaching at a subsistence wage would be a waste of time. When none of his hopes for a well-paying position was fulfilled, he reconsidered the Harvard Divinity School. Upon receiving considerable encouragement and offers of financial aid, Frank paid a visit to Professor Huntington, who in turn took Abbot's case anonymously to Dr. Convers Francis of the Divinity School. Later Abbot discussed his plight with not only Professors Francis and Noyes but also with President Walker. "They all declared my marriage no impediment to taking this step." He also declared that Dr. Walker's sermon the previous Sunday on Christ the one Mediator "finally quelled my skeptical doubts, and I feel strong to bear all *truthfully* and *cheerfully* that my dear Savior shall lay upon me. My cross will become my stay and support, if He is with me."[2]

The doubts of which Abbot speaks illuminate complexities in Boston Unitarianism at mid-century that are often overlooked. These doubts may well have been stimulated by Professor Huntington's decision to be confirmed in the Episcopal Church, and later the decision of his dear friend William Huntington to join their mentor in his move. Nothing demonstrates the fundamentally evangelical nature of Unitarianism in the mid-1850s more than the response of Abbot and others to the confirmation of William Huntington. Charles W. Eliot, who was later to become the famous president of Harvard, but then was an assistant professor, wrote to Abbot: "I was very sorry to hear what you told me about your classmate Huntington—he is such a very nice fellow that he ought to belong to the liberal Clergy—he has been too much under one set of influences, it seems to me. If you were in Cambridge could you not give him a twist in the right direction?"[3] But far from being prepared to "twist" William Huntington, Abbot seems to have wondered if he should not follow his mentor down the Trinitarian path. A letter from Professor Huntington reveals that this alternative had been seriously considered.

My dear friend, since you were here on Sat. it has occurred to me

---

[2]FEA to Katie, 25 October 1859. The sermon "The Mediator," contained in Walker's *Sermons* (Boston, 1861), was a conservative Unitarian interpretation that emphasized the divine and special mission of Christ.

[3]Eliot to FEA, 28 September 1859. See the volume published by the American Unitarian Association as an answer to Huntington's change of mind: *The New Discussion of the Trinity: Containing Notices of Professor Huntington's Recent Defense of That Doctrine* (Boston, 1860).

more than once that there was something unsaid then and all along
which ought to be said. Perhaps you understand it already. The cor-
dial, happy & sacred relations which have grown up betw. us forbid
that there sh'd be any ambiguity in my attitude towards any of y'r
plans. It is of importance to me to avoid that: & this is the chief motive as you will presently understand, of my writing.

   You mentioned yr purpose of entering the Cambridge Divinity
School, & of availing y'rself of the Funds there. Without concluding
from this that you will then express a definite purpose to become ultimately a Unitarian minister, I suppose it is fair to infer that y'r
present general intention is to preach under some [one] of the great
[variety] of forms of belief which bear that name. What I w'd say is,
this, for reasons which it w'd require a long time to state, which lie
very deep in my convictions & my heart, & which have exerted their
power upon me [at great cost], I am not able to feel a sympathy with
such a plan. You will not expect it of me. I always expect to feel an
interest and confidence *in you*. And—as I told you—if I ever hear of
any pupils for you, I shall at once let you know.

   It is hard to refrain from saying more. My hopes, wishes, affec-
tions & faith—dear & strong—urge it. But it is not best. God bless
you! Christ lead you! The Holy Spirit direct you! away from all error
and into all truth.[4]

Being convinced that he could be both a Unitarian and a believer in
the saving grace of Christ, Abbot rejected the lure of Trinitarianism
and finally decided to enter the Unitarian ministry.

   "In October Mr. Frank E. Abbot became a member of the Junior
Class," states the students' record. Frank also carried out the long-
discussed plan for making their marriage public in the Boston papers
and found that his fears of there being a deluge of gossip were insub-
stantial. Before long people were much more excited about a student named Forbes who almost killed a night-watchman; the problems
and controversy connected with the resignation of President Walker;
and the transfer to the Episcopal clergy of Professor Huntington.

   Frank's academic duties were apparently not overly arduous. He
gained a reputation as a conservative and as an organizer of devotional meetings. He also undertook a wide gamut of outside activities.
First of all, Frank volunteered to take a class of boys, "chiefly Irish,"
in the evening charity school. This school was located at the Pitts
Street Chapel and maintained by the Reverend Edmund Squire of
the Washington Village Church (in what was then Dorchester). He also

---

[4]Huntington to FEA, 12 September 1859.

agreed to teach five hours of arithmetic and chemistry a week at a Mrs. Comegy's English and French Boarding School for Young Ladies in Cambridge. This too turned out to be partly a charity venture since the mistress defaulted in her payments. Frank was made a proctor of an entry in Hollis Hall, and in December he took on a private pupil— "a son of Gerrit Smith's [and] a very pleasant fellow"—to whom he gave Greek and Latin lessons while his brother Edwin handled the other subjects.

It was under those circumstances that Frank pursued his studies of Unitarian divinity and pastoral care, taking a "miserly view" of the passing minutes. His extracurricular reading had to be postponed until winter vacation, when he stayed in his "metaphysical den" at the college. There Abbot spent three hours a morning with his pupil and the rest of the day with his books. These studies were for a critical examination of Sir William Hamilton's philosophy of the "Unconditioned" that Abbot was writing with a view toward publication in the *North American Review*. He undertook this perhaps to balance the "trash" he was writing for *Ballou's Pictorial and Drawing-Room Companion*.[5]

The year taken as a whole was a dismal, trying one, with only a rare public gathering of some sort or occasional parties with friends to break the monotony. Abbot's time as a Harvard theological student would be remembered as one of drudgery and frugality.

In the meantime Katie was hardly revelling in Arcadia. "My chamber is like a barn," she wrote, "the wind comes in so round the window that the curtain blows all the time." Moreover, she could not even go to church as she wished. "If you had ever been to a Methodist or Baptist Church out west you would not wonder at my not wishing to go to either, and I do not feel as if I ought to walk as far as I should be obliged to if I went to the Episcopal or Congregational." Finally, on 14 May 1860, Katie gave birth to a baby girl named Ethel.[6]

Spring turned into a beautiful summer; Frank added pupils that promised to net him $200 during vacation; and on 27 July he took his brother Edwin's advice and went on a vacation. Abbot returned to find a tragic note from Katie—reporting that their child had died of chol-

---

[5]The articles on the Scottish philosopher Hamilton, which were not published until 1864, will be discussed in the section devoted to Abbot's developing philosophy and theology. Regarding his own assessment of his writings for *Ballou's Companion,* see FEA to Katie, 18 February 1860.

[6]Katie to FEA, 13 November 1859.

era. The way the tragedy shook Frank's spirit is best revealed in the
letter he wrote Katie on their first wedding anniversary.

My noble, darling wife—

What shall I say to you, what prayer shall I send up for you to our
Father's throne, to still the agony of your little heart. My poor little
wife! Would God, would God I could bear the burden of both! Oh how
my soul is rent with fear and anguish for you, poor childless mother!
May God be near you, and fill you with all soothing peace and trust!
Dearest, dearest, dearest little Katie, my own, own darling, do not
grieve your life away, do not let the tearless agony crush your suffering spirit, for your mission to my selfish heart is not ended yet. Live
still, live still to lift me nearer God with the brave, filial submission
of a piety whose depths I never knew till now. The little angel in our
Father's bosom will watch our faltering steps, will draw down bless-
ings unnumbered on our stricken heads, and heaven will be closer now
that earth has lost its charm. Lead me on, holy soul, pure, loving, God-
given wife of my bosom, my all, my angel on earth; when in the bitterness of bereavement, a bitterness that has no equal, you still only
think of consoling me, of rejoicing in the blessedness of our little Ethel,
my soul bows down into the dust, and I must kneel beside you in
prayer to God, feeling that He who has sent me such an angel by my
side will keep the lost angel safe until our coming. . . . One year ago,
my darling, one year ago today, you gave me your heart and hand
and soul. And thus has our Father seen fit that I should celebrate the
day of anniversary.

Up, broken heart, up, look up to God, and know that your darling's eyes are looking up with you; and our Ethel shall gaze down on
us from our Father's arms.

Lovingly your own,

Frank.[7]

In the meantime Katie was faring ill and her sister begged Frank
to make some arrangement to end the separation. Shortly after, a tear-
stained letter from Katie made action imperative: "Oh Frank, Frank,
it seems sometimes more than I can bear! The loss of my baby, and
this separation from you! In one short year I have been a wife, a
mother, and now I am childless, and far away from you, my darling.
Surely ours has been no easy lot." Facing such a cry, Abbot immediately investigated a position in a girls' seminary in Meadville,
Pennsylvania. Here he could teach and serve as principal while attending divinity school part time. George Chaney, his classmate, who

[7]FEA to Katie, 3 August 1860.

was studying divinity there under a similar arrangement, had long been urging this, and he was instrumental in convincing the necessary people that Frank should be hired. In September, after many delays, word came that the job was his. Almost immediately Frank set out for Meadville. Since Frank and Katie could not foresee that life in Meadville would be as painful and arduous as any in the past had been, there is no way of calculating how they felt on the 18th of October, Katie's birthday, when Frank carried all eighty-nine pounds of her over their first threshold.

When Frank Abbot waved good-bye to his father in Boston station and "whirled off in the cars" it was no sudden happenstance that had made his destination Meadville. A number of Harvard associates had regaled him with lyrical accounts of the town and the theological school, while every visitor described Meadville's fertile countryside and industrious populace. An anonymous brochure explains how "the moisture generated from Lake Erie in hot weather gives to the forests and fields . . . the same wealth of verdure that is characteristic of western New York." Although Meadville was the seat of Crawford County and growing steadily, it was not a large town, having a population of only 2,578 in 1850 and 3,702 in 1860. Politically, these people were much influenced by a large black element and the proximity of Virginia, Kentucky, and the Ohio valley. Presbyterians and Congregationalists were dominant. Considering that in 1850 there were not two thousand Unitarians in the whole state, it was somewhat extraordinary that this distant outpost, located in the very heartland of Calvinistic orthodoxy and frontier revivalism, should have become a western center of Boston's liberal theology.[8]

In 1844 a liberal, nondenominational theological school was founded to bolster the small Unitarian community. This was done with the outward cooperation of the anti-Calvinistic "Christian Denomination," but it was essentially a Unitarian project. An old Cumberland Presbyterian church was bought and refitted to provide a chapel, library, and classroom. The American Unitarian Association, which had long entertained plans for a Western seminary, promised annual aid, and later the Reverend Rufus Phineas Stebbins of Leominster,

---

[8]*Meadville, Pa.* (Meadville, c. 1864) 1. This brochure was published under Unitarian auspices.

Massachusetts, agreed to be president of the new institution and minister to the Meadville Society.[9]

Stebbins was a conservative Unitarian, a follower of Andrews Norton, and an advocate of traditional theology based on Joseph Butler's *Analogy of Religion* and William Paley's *Evidences of Christianity,* and summed up in John Gorham Palfrey's Lowell lectures. His theological outlook is aptly characterized by the title of his address to the Harvard Divinity School in 1852, "The Bible: the Authoritative Rule of Faith and Practice." He was oblivious to the new biblical criticism, scornful of anything "Transcendental," a defender of Edwards Amasa Park of Andover, and friendly to the evangelistic currents of the West. Stebbins was a man who, as he said it, "[belonged] to the old fashioned class of persons who believed that piety, a devout religious spirit, is as necessary to clear perception of the truths of theology as logical acuteness and vigorous ratiocination." It was the Stebbins regime that earned Theodore Parker's withering observation: "The Egyptian embalmers took only seventy days, I think, to make a mummy out of a dead man. Unitarian embalmers [at the Harvard Divinity School] use three years in making a mummy out of live men. I think at Meadville they do it in less."[10] During the ten years of his direction, the school nevertheless grew considerably in size and influence.

The Reverend Oliver Stearns came to the presidency in 1856, bringing to the school a spirit that revealed contact with a newer conception of science and evolutionary philosophy. Stearns was the central figure of the school when Abbot came to Meadville; he was then professor of theology, ethics, and biblical literature. Despite this apparent turn, Abbot found himself out of step at Meadville, and suffering financially. Frank had planned to support himself and Katie by his duties at the girls' academy, yet his plans eventually ran aground. Criticism by orthodox elements of the town made the school's Unitarian sponsorship increasingly suspect. Furthermore, Abbot's political leanings did not help matters any. As was true of many Northerners with a driving sense of moral principle, he was an outspoken supporter of the Radical Republicans and of racial equality. Neither view was popular among the doughface populace.[11]

---

[9]Francis A. Christie, *The Makers of Meadville Theological School, 1844-1894* (Boston: Beacon Press, 1927) 1-24.

[10]Ibid., 39.

[11]FEA to Father, 1 June 1862; FEA to Chaney, 23 November 1862.

Accordingly, Frank's financial difficulties became increasingly grave. The salary he promised to pay an assistant teacher proved to be more than he could afford; the express company overcharged him for his move west; a former employer from Cambridge failed to pay his back salary; a college debtor fled his obligations; no one could be found to sublet his room at the Harvard Divinity School; nor did the fifty cents received for a poem accepted by the *Monthly Religious Magazine* alleviate the situation. For 1861-1862 Frank obtained the services of his Harvard friend, George Chaney, as a mathematics instructor and worked out, after tedious negotiations, an arrangement for his sister Emily to be his assistant in drawing and other subjects. But when autumn came Abbot still found it necessary to bolster his income by tutoring additional students. All in all, the work, the loneliness, the bitterness of controversy, and anxiety over his two brothers in the Union army made his years in Meadville a time of many personal trials such as he hoped never to know again.

> My existence comes as near the ideal of stagnation as any barn-yard puddle. . . . You cannot have half understood the isolation which has gripped me this year, and nearly squeezed the soul out of me. In fact, the deviltry of my year's existence has concentrated, the last few months, into the quintessence of all I hate. . . . I think another year like the last would irrevocably break me down, and Katie too. Thank God, the end is near.[12]

Abbot's three years at Meadville—despite their frustration, pain, and monotony—were nevertheless important ones in his intellectual development, and the influences that came to bear upon him were forceful and profound. Frank's lack of a teaching load allowed him to spend more time with his studies and even allowed him to be a full-time student in 1862-1863. Formal schooling brought changes in his schedule: three times a week the long lectures of Dr. Stearns, classes, weekly religious meetings at the school, and on Wednesday evenings the student sermons. Frank delivered his first sermon on the "Knowledge of God" in September of 1862. The following March he formally entered a Unitarian pulpit for the first time, as a substitute for the minister to the Meadville Society. During 1861-1862 he had been meeting regularly with Dr. Stearns and had done the required reading and written work. With his accredited year at Harvard, this entitled Abbot to a ministerial certificate the following June (1863). The *Catalogue* for 1862-1863 lists a wide gamut of study for the senior

---

[12]FEA to Chaney, 31 May; 27 January; 8 June 1863.

class. First Term: Old Testament literature and interpretation, ethics, systematic theology, exegesis of the "latter Epistles," and homiletics; Second Term: homiletics and ethics (continued), the Apocalypse, New Testament exegesis, church government and services, and pastoral care. On a more profound level, these years marked a transition to adulthood. Only in the days of torment following his assumption of adult responsibilities did he sense the meaning of maturity: "I feel ten years older," he had remarked in the autumn of 1859. By any such calculation, Meadville had added another ten.

More specific influences during this time include the strength Chaney gave to Abbot's Christian faith. Chaney's impact was felt during Frank's second year, at which time Chaney was both an associate and boarder—"a member of the family." Until death Chaney remained one of Frank's closest friends. Chaney was a resolute conservative in theology then and remained so all of his life. More than any other in those years, his example kept Frank striving for the devotional, Christian life. Of almost equal significance was the Reverend Richard Metcalf, the Unitarian minister. Metcalf, too, was a theological conservative who in 1868 was to upbraid the National Conference for its liberalism whereas Frank, by then, had revolted from its "authoritarianism." In the last analysis, however, neither friend prevailed: "If I could only live in the spirit with Jesus the sharpest sting would be gone," wrote Frank in the dreary summer of 1862, "but I can not."[13]

But as Abbot's confidence in evangelical Unitarianism began to wane, a new interest began to grow. "I have acquired a taste for science," he remarked only a fortnight later, thus indicating the corollary to his religious difficulties.[14] However much this may have represented a true acceptance of his father's scientific interest, it was a distinct departure from his own past attitude and the most significant intellectual transition of the Meadville years. Although Frank received a 32-point "deduction" for cheering the final class of Asa Gray, there is little other evidence that science aroused his enthusiasm at Harvard. Abbot ranked consistently much lower than classmates in all of his science courses and he openly rejoiced when he finally was able to drop mathematics. What led Abbot to realize the significance of the method that he had formerly spurned was his firsthand experience with it as a teacher; the important influence of Pres-

---

[13]Ibid., 4 August 1862.
[14]FEA to Father, 17 August 1862.

ident Stearns and George L. Cary; and the studies he was pursuing with regard to his critique of Scottish philosopher William Hamilton.

The long, private conferences with Stearns, as well as formal academic contacts, made an important impression on Abbot. Though in many respects a traditional Unitarian, Stearns was a rationalist at heart: "No authority can uphold that which has no basis in the rational constitution of man," he insisted.[15] Moreover, he was willing to accept God's immanence in nature and in humanity, thus leaving a place for a somewhat ambiguously defined "religious intuition" of divine truth. Stearns was also in tune with the scientific spirit of his time, which was shaped by Baconian method: "To know . . . is to commune through the medium of fact and truth with God himself. It is to experience finitely what Deity experiences infinitely."[16] Influenced by the protégé of Louis Agassiz, Professor Arnold Henry Guyot, and Ernst von Baer, Stearns was "probably the first academic theologian in America to announce a belief in evolution as a universal cosmic law." At the same time Abbot was always deeply moved by what he called "the great spiritual power" of Stearns.[17]

Cary, who spent a whole year as a boarder in the Abbot household, was also important. He was equally interested in science: one of his most serious projects was to unite, in a logical structure, all scientific knowledge—a "Scheme of Pantology," as he called it.[18] Although Cary later became best known for work in New Testament criticism, he also taught logic, psychology, and Hamilton's metaphysics in his earlier years. Similarly inspired by this "scientific" emphasis were Abbot's closest student friends after George Chaney: Charles W. Buck, A. W. Stevens, and Everett Finley. Not all of them traveled as far down the road as Abbot did, but in Meadville they supported each other in their collective drift toward a liberalism that was uncongenial to orthodox Unitarians.

Under such auspices Abbot became enthusiastic about scientific methodology and developed an avid interest in the progress of the inductive sciences. This interest was further kindled as Abbot worked

---

[15]Harvard Divinity School Address, *Christian Examiner,* September 1853; cited in Christie, *Makers,* 83. But this must be understood in contradistinction to the views revealed in *The Incarnation: A Sermon Preached at the Ordination of Rev. C. S. Locke* (Boston, 1855).

[16]*Knowledge: Its Relation to the Progress of Mankind* (Hingham, 1852).

[17]Christie, *Makers,* 79; FEA to Anne Mumford, 30 July 1866.

[18]Ibid., 120.

on his critique of Hamilton's agnosticism. Hamilton, following Kant, argued that human beings could have no true knowledge of the world in itself. For Abbot, this undermined both religion and science. During this time Frank even began to lament his deficient knowledge of mathematics. His attack on Hamilton was but the first indication of a lifelong desire to use scientific method to escape agnosticism.

Out of the drudgery of teaching, the unending demands for study, ideological conflict, and financial duress Abbot discovered his true nature, or at least those aspects of himself that were to dominate his future career. In youth his interests had been poetic, though even as a twelve-year-old he had written strangely metaphysical poetry; however, during Frank's last two years of college his religious interests had asserted themselves through the turmoil of his problems of conscience. The love songs and funereal lamentations became hymns, and the career of pastor became his ambition. At Meadville Abbot made one more shift, from theology to philosophy, or from faith to reason. Religious he had always been, and so he always remained; but during these years his religion took on a cast of thought which, if it was pale at first, deepened gradually as its logical implications became clear to him. Already in his first sermon, preached to the divinity students in September 1862, one can discern the "scientific theism" that was to become "a radical's theology."[19]

At the same time one can observe Frank's increasing resistance to any thought or action that suggested the priority of "policy" over "principle." He also struggled against the lure of "success" and all "authoritarian" limitations on intellectual freedom. Although only premonitory in their first manifestations, these attitudes form an important pattern. Whether or not he was seeking a rationalization for failures such as the private school in Meadville, one cannot say; but it is true that his outlook offered a safe haven from the pragmatic problems of the world. Abbot always took the "higher ground," obeyed the "higher law"; the men of the world became his oppressors. With "absolute freedom" as his slogan, Abbot separated himself from all men. All of his suppressed aggressions, all of his insecurity, found expression in the battle he fought under that standard. The motives and wisdom of even his closest cohorts were impugned. Abbot made himself the persecuted one. In his world there were lonely, painful victories.

---

[19]The sermon "The Knowledge of God" reflected the attitude described in a letter to Chaney (2 November 1862): "What limitless value I place on scientific and abstract truth, religious in nature and philosophic in method!"

Already at Meadville Abbot had begun to view the powers of the world as in league against the cause of truth. The Divinity School in Cambridge, he said, was acting to decimate a rival when it offered a chair to Dr. Stearns. The Meadville Theological School was bowing to worldly motives in asking Dr. William H. Furness of Philadelphia to be class speaker, since it believed that his influence would aid the institution. As Abbot faced the prospect of ordination, his fear of ecclesiastical encroachment anticipated the major struggles of his later years. What he called his "Reverential Radicalism" was already formed, and he was determined neither to join or be joined by any "party."[20]

As to the authority of any council of ministers to control his settlement as a minister, "I have made up my mind not to comply with it, even at the risk of not being allowed to preach. . . . I never will consent to be interrogated on such points, unless a congregation with a thought of inviting me should desire information for itself. Nobody else has any business with my opinions." Disappointments had been many and comforts few in Meadville. Frank had checked off the remaining years and months as a prisoner in confinement would. Graduation meant release. Commencement ceremonies on "Anniversary Day," 25 June 1863, were an occasion for thanksgiving, not celebration. With all possible haste he closed his affairs and departed, to begin the task of candidating, or seeking a congregation that would call him as their minister. He realized, however, that with his radical religious views this would be no easy goal.[21]

---

[20]FEA to Chaney, 8 February 1863.

[21]Ibid.

CHAPTER FOUR

THE MINISTRY AT DOVER

THE LAST NOTES of the hymn Abbot had written for the graduation ceremony of the Meadville Theological School had hardly died away before he began preparations for departure. In less than two weeks he had taken his wife through Chicago to the Mississippi River (whence she went by riverboat up to Winona), while he returned to Detroit and began candidating in the Unitarian Society there. Candidating involved a trial period of several weeks during which a prospective minister would preach to a congregation, and after which they would determine whether or not to call him. Sweltering in an uncommonly hot summer, and suffering with colic, Frank was living in a boardinghouse. He shared a room with a young Baptist minister who, though affable, "was not an agreeable bed-fellow."[1]

Almost immediately Abbot performed his first funeral service. The funeral was held for a corporal killed at Gettysburg, and Frank found it "a new and solemn experience." "The Lord loveth a cheerful giver" was his text. Just a few days later the text as well as that terrible battle took on more personal meaning.

> My young brother Stanley is dead. . . . As I wrote you he was wounded at the battle of Gettysburg, being shot in the right breast; and the surgeon told him the wound was not mortal . . . on July 8 his breath grew shorter and shorter, and finally ceased. . . . Edwin did not reach the Hospital until he had been dead two days; they had laid him under the grass on the hillside, beneath the trees, and on the bank of a little brook, the only peaceful spot in the midst of infinite turmoil and confusion. . . . Stanley did not suffer much pain and was very happy at the thought of dying for his country.[2]

Regarding the society for which Abbot was at least theoretically a candidate, he was from the first uninterested.

They want a man, it seems, who will fill the house, and not preach

---

[1]FEA to Katie, 5 and 15 July 1863.
[2]Ibid., 20 July 1863.

abolition too hotly. I am not fanatic, but I would die, and be damned too, before I would mortgage my tongue. . . . I never will preach anywhere to fill up empty pews. . . . I hanker more than ever for the East again [he wrote later from Winona]. I hope for some little quiet parish near Boston and my friends. . . . I cannot yet contemplate with equanimity the thought of living in the West.[3]

But he was no better satisfied with his own abilities: "I have sounded my ministerial capacity and mortifyingly touch bottom very soon," he wrote to Chaney. Abbot found himself bored by and inept in the social arts, and his stammer interfered seriously with his preaching. His associations with parishioners were limited; the response to his message seemed small. The time passed slowly and painfully, and pleasures were few. Only an occasional fugitive compliment came his way. "I hear great satisfaction expressed on every hand," he reported ironically. "Somebody said that somebody said that somebody said that I was original! That's Fame, Katie!" Nor did Frank seem to have underestimated their enthusiasm. For six Sunday mornings he read, without display, one from his slowly growing collection of carefully written sermons; and on evenings when the weather was not insufferable, Frank extemporized at more informal meetings. The society listened to Abbot's advanced views and strong convictions and decided to look elsewhere for their pastor.[4]

In October of 1863 Frank began "candidating" in the East. For eight arduous months he made his rounds, preaching for greater or lesser periods, at more than a dozen societies from Yonkers, New York, to Concord, New Hampshire. Katie had become pregnant and Edward Stanley was born 13 December 1863. At this time Frank and Katie could not afford to establish a home. Katie shuttled between Beverly and her sister's home in Concord; Frank lived from a suitcase in distant parishes. "A more killing, murdering, deadening, existence cannot be conceived than that of candidate," he later declared, but by that time the ordeal was over. The Dover, New Hampshire, society had unanimously issued a call to him, and though only a $1000 living was offered, Abbot accepted: "Not a dazzling offer; but that is not what I want." He could now look forward to a home, a parish, and perhaps

---

[3]Ibid., 5 July 1863.
[4]Ibid., 29 July 1863; FEA to Chaney, 24 August 1863.

the fulfillment of a collegiate hope "for a calm and uneventful life with my little fairy mignon."[5]

A calm and uneventful life, however, did not lie in the future for either Abbot or this small Unitarian society. For a few stormy years, this far-removed town on the Cocheco was a center of religious radicalism; the conflict within its Unitarian society, which finally reached the state supreme court, was anxiously observed and discussed by conservatives and radicals alike; and the minister to the parish became one of the leaders of the American Free Religious movement.

The grueling eight months as itinerant preacher had not precluded active thought; the constant need for new sermons, in fact, had stimulated Abbot's religious thinking. The period does not, however, reveal any startling changes in outlook, only a continuation of his drift toward theological "positivism." Frank's two articles, the product of such concentrated effort over a three-year period, were finally published in the *North American Review;* they documented his philosophical repudiation of Sir William Hamilton. Abbot's sermons, at the same time, reveal him to be still in the grip of what a friend, Edward C. Towne, called "Jesusism," or the attempt to balance increasingly radical religious insight with the continuity of traditional language. Abbot's humanistic interpretation of Christ's mission was still veiled in eulogistic terminology. "The life of Jesus is the one great marvel of history," he said in a sermon composed at Beverly in April 1864. "Christ . . . is purely human [but] . . . he has forever proved the possibility of a god-like life on earth." Abbot had reached the outside limit of "liberal Christianity." Even disrobed of euphemism a certain faith remained; Jesus is still *the one great marvel.*" In all other respects the Christ of the Gospels had become the ethical teacher and example, the "giver of peace." Abbot spoke of "our Master and Lord, our Savior and Redeemer," and he urged men to let their lives be "hid with Christ in God." All of the terms he was using had taken on a naturalistic meaning by now. How many parishioners in Dover had really penetrated his vocabulary, no one could say; it remained to be seen

---

[5]FEA to Chaney, 16 June 1864. Edward Stanley was the second child of Frank and Katie. Another son, Everett Vergnies, had been born earlier in 1862. One final child, Fanny Larcom, would be born in 1872. In addition to these three, five other children were to die in infancy, which contributed greatly to Katie's declining health.

what reaction would follow the gradual stripping away of pious phraseology.[6]

Late in August 1864, after all was in readiness, Frank called his family to his new Dover parsonage. The location was not ideal, and they would later become offended by the vile pigpen and the stables nearby; but the house had been generously furnished by various parishioners. The final plans for the ordination were all that remained to do. The ceremony occurred in August 1864, without any questions about doctrine, despite Abbot's continuing theological concern for the authority of the ordaining council. Abbot probably would not have yielded to ordination had it not been for the assurance of his kinsman, Edward Everett Hale, who said that he did "not attach the slightest importance to the presence or organization of a Council, except as I am glad to see others besides clergymen actively called upon in all such affairs." He went on to say that it was necessary, moreover, if Abbot was to have an ordination that was "perfectly valid," that would "stand in law" as conferring the right to perform marriages; it was merely a confirmatory action.[7]

With such modest duties his council convened on the morning of 31 August only to read the exchange of correspondence between Abbot and the parish and to ratify the proceedings. Not a word was said about doctrine. The public service in the afternoon, on the other hand, was an assembly of notables as well as talents, and the society members who listened to the fourteen numbers on the program must have thought that things augured well. The program featured not only many of Frank's friends but some of the most prominent Unitarian leaders. James Freeman Clarke, the moderate Transcendentalist and antislavery advocate, delivered the sermon and Edward Everett Hale the charge. Most of the others were college or Divinity School associates. George Chaney extended the right hand of fellowship and after the ceremony baptized the Abbots' children.

Dover in the 1860s was not just another peaceful New England village. These were years of transition during which the town was adjusting itself to the pressures of expansion and the new immigration. In 1820 it had been a homogeneous community of 2,871 people,

---

[6]Sermon no. 14, "The Mission of Jesus," Matt. 22:42, "What think ye of the Christ?" Written 22 April 1864, but never read to a society after 1864. See also sermons nos. 6, 20, and 10, none of which was used after 1864.

[7]Hale to FEA, 27 August 1864. Regarding Abbot's theological concerns, see FEA to Chaney, 23 August 1864.

served religiously only by the established Congregational church. The decade following wrenched it from rural ways. The Cocheco [cotton] Manufacturing Company expanded into a million-dollar enterprise, and Sawyer Woolen Mills was founded in 1824. By 1830 the population had doubled to 5,549 and the increase had made itself felt on the religious structure of the town. New churches were founded: the Methodist Episcopal (1824), the Universalist (1825), Free Will Baptist (1826), Catholic (1826), "Regular" Baptist (1827), and Unitarian (1827). It was in 1832 that Episcopalian services were first held. After this relatively sudden expansion the growth continued more slowly. Rail connections were established in 1842, and by 1845 there was a direct line to Boston. In 1855 village government was replaced by "city" government. By 1860 the population had reached 8,502.

The place of the Unitarians in this development seems fairly clear. Nearly all of them were of Yankee stock; many of them had moved into the city from Boston as various enterprises were established; and a large number of the town's entrepreneurs were in the society. That a small group of such men should band together for a society and erect a large, impressive brick church that could only very rarely be filled suggests their affluence. The later state of the society tells something of the religious ardor of their successors. In 1862, when these men accepted a request from their minister to be given nine months' leave for chaplain service, they voted as well "to close the church on and after the first Sunday in November next, and, to keep it closed until the debts of the society are liquidated[!]" It is no wonder that Abbot described his parishioners as "nice people, some of them perfectly splendid, but most of them good, quiet, inert Christians, with kind hearts and infinitesimal zeal."[8]

Nor was Abbot the type who could be expected to correct such a state of affairs. He had insisted in Detroit that he would not be a "society-builder." Moreover, he had "almost no young men" in his parish, and as he remarked, "I can do nothing for old people." There is no evidence that he ever softened the rigor of his logic in order to appease or attract anybody. As for changing his message to avoid criticism or win favor, that was out of the question: "I make no plea for

---

[8]FEA to Chaney, 19 October 1864. Regarding the growth of Dover, see Durer J. H. Ward, *Unitarianism in Dover, New Hampshire* (Denver CO: Up the Divide Publishing Co., 1926); and George Wadleigh, *Notable Events in the History of Dover* (Dover NH, 1913).

liberty," Abbot said. "I would not accept as a favor what I demand as a right."[9]

But he was not completely unsuccessful. The Dover *Gazette,* the more liberal of the town's two major papers, referred to his "peculiar style of reasoning, good but oftentimes quaint," and gave extended reviews of his sermons. *The Gazette* frequently advised its readers that Abbot's ideas merited "serious perusal." During the first year, at least, Abbot several times reported that nearly 700 people had quite filled the church.[10]

On political matters Abbot was zealous, but he emerged virtually unscathed. Dover was quite equally divided along political party lines, with the *Gazette* being Democratic and the *Enquirer* Republican. In 1864 Lincoln carried Dover only by an 863 to 569 margin. But the Unitarian society contained "only three Copperheads." Thus there was no great dissent when their pastor spent election day passing out Lincoln literature, or when, after the election, he hung out two little flags "in honor of our grand victory over the Devil and his angels."[11]

Yet criticism did come and factions arose to disrupt the society. The issue was Abbot's radical theology, which, though neither explicit nor extreme during the first year, became increasingly pronounced thereafter. His predecessor, the Reverend Edwin M. Wheelock, had held similar views; yet he had not possessed Abbot's determination to state his views bluntly and explicitly, without the slightest cover of euphemism.[12] More important, perhaps, Wheelock had not the stimulus to radicalism provided by the conservative resolutions and enactments of the first convention of the National Unitarian Conference. Since this larger issue is discussed in a later chapter, only brief mention need be made here of the difficulty. It arose because the adopted constitution of the National Conference contained an explicit Christian affirmation. Abbot had been silent in the debates on the subject, but he had been perturbed by the results. His sermon reporting to the society the actions of the conference was critical of some of the conference's actions, and thereafter he became de-

---

[9]Regarding the self-assessment, see FEA to Anne Mumford, 25 May 1865; Sermon no. 49, "Radicalism," 30 July 1865.

[10]Dover *Gazette,* 13 March 1868.

[11]FEA to Chaney, 9 November 1864.

[12]See, e.g., Wheelock's *Inspiration* (Boston, 1857), which attacked the habit of singling out the Bible as the only inspired book.

termined to elucidate clearly a radical position. In July Abbot preached
a sermon on "The Authority of Jesus," and argued,

> There can be for us no such thing as an authority superior to our own
> individual reason. . . . When, therefore, we hear it said that Chris-
> tianity rests on the authority of Christ or of the Bible, we may be as-
> sured that neither Christ nor the Bible makes this impossible claim.
> . . . They simply strove to awake the sleepy soul. . . . The soul must
> be its own base. We cannot anchor to any infallible book or infallible
> teacher. . . . [He went on to say that nobody does take the Bible lit-
> erally, and from this, that it is not *really* an authority.] *I find no com-
> fort,* strength, or help, in those sayings of Christ which I cannot myself
> see to be true. . . . Some of Christ's sayings I am compelled to doubt,
> and some to disbelieve. . . . I believe, then, that Christ has no au-
> thority whatever over our reason. [Thus, he concluded] . . . the yoke
> of this authority is easy, and its burden light.[13]

The outcry was not long in coming: the "rumblings" of which he
had heard intimations soon broke into print. It became apparent that
"a great ferment was taking place in certain quarters." Benjamin
Barnes, Jr. of the Dover *Mirror* led the assault. He attacked Abbot by
printing certain excerpts from a manuscript of the sermon, which he
obtained without Abbot's permission. An acrimonious correspondence followed, with Barnes commenting on the disposition of the society in a way that boded ill for the future. Barnes admitted
Wheelock's liberalism, then proceeded to his critique of Abbot and a
call for a "return of good old-fashioned Unitarian preaching—more
faith, less scepticism, more trust in Christ, the Lord and Savior and
less doubt as to his mission." On this particular occasion Abbot closed
off the affair with a terse and particularly acerbic letter, but Barnes
was ultimately to organize the silent majority of Channing-Norton
Christians of the society.[14]

The effect on Abbot was perhaps the opposite of what Barnes
hoped for, since his sermons became even more outspoken, as was revealed by his final sermon of the year on "The Issue of the Age."

> The question is this:—What reason shall we give for the hope that is
> in us? . . . I side wholly and unequivocally with Reason. . . . We have
> no infallible authority whatever. [He then went on to assail dogmatic
> atheism, pantheism, and negative atheism like Spencer's. But he saw
> no conflict with science.] Theology starts from the soul, as part of the

---

[13]Sermon no. 48, "The Authority of Jesus," delivered 16 July 1865.

[14]Benjamin Barnes to FEA, 5 August 1865.

spiritual universe, and by a strictly scientific examination of its nature, capacities, and tendencies, arrives at the two great truths of im-
mortality and God.[15]

His return from the second meeting of the National Unitarian
Conference (10 and 11 October 1866) found Abbot more determined
than ever to fight the "authoritarians." Abbot's main energies now
turned to the issues of national Unitarianism and the Free Religious
Association. An immense correspondence began to take priority over
parochial duties. While a small group in the society delighted that their
minister was a leader of radicalism, the majority, who were in no mood
to reward heresy, registered their displeasure by staying away from
services and neglecting to support the church. At the end of 1866, with
expenses running $400 ahead of the salary he received, Frank was
obliged to ask for an increase; but at a parish meeting in which dissatisfaction was openly expressed, it was voted down. The women of
the parish got up a levee and held a number of parties through which
nearly $300 was raised, but this was only a gesture. This coupled with
the ill-health of his wife after the death of another baby girl, and other
personal woes, all contributed to the most agonizing year Frank was
to remember.

Early in 1867, in the midst of this gloomy period, Abbot began
seeking an academic position. Although never having met Horace
Bushnell, the great preacher-theologian, Abbot wrote to him asking
for his assistance in securing such a position. Bushnell's negative response illumines the philosophical gulf separating the generation of
the Transcendentalists from the new scientific, theistic world of Abbot. Words, not metaphysics, interested Bushnell.

After anyone has gotten the insight of words, where all true intelligence (*intus lego*) centres and comes to its limits, I do not think it possible for him to care much for logic and metaphysics. He has
discovered by that time the possibility of systems without end, and
the impossibility of any that can stand. And it is a fact not to be questioned, that metaphysics have never established anything. . . . There
is in fact no science here, and never will be,—language is too light-
winged and too competent of right uses to be harnessed in this mill.[16]

---

[15]Sermon no. 62, 31 December 1865.

[16]See [Mary A. B. Chaney, ed.,] *Life and Letters of Horace Bushnell* (New
York: Harper and Bros., 1903) 492-94.

Reading between the lines of this letter one can perhaps see the seeds of Abbot's later rejection of not merely orthodox Christianity but even Transcendentalism.

In early November, upon receiving word that his application for a professorial appointment at Cornell was being passed by, Abbot requested the society's permission to spend his weekdays in Cambridge, coming to Dover only on Sundays. When the request was granted, he took up rooms near Harvard and applied (not too hopefully) for a spring term proctorship. Frank also began work on certain reviews for the *North American Review* that Charles Eliot Norton had asked for and a revision of his "Ministerial Union Address" for the *Christian Examiner*. But dissatisfaction in his church mounted, people strode out of services during his sermons or stayed away altogether, and an increasingly strong resistance to his diverse outside activities manifested itself. He finally decided to abandon Dover, since "the chairman of the wardens of my Society informed me last week, that the character of my theology is so distasteful to many of my people that it is impossible to raise above four-fifths of my small salary of $1000."[17]

These were days of gloom. Abbot's theology had stripped Christmas of religious significance and now the facts of a bare and crushing existence seemed to rob it of earthly joy. But when the day came, his past "suddenly came to wear a very different look": a Christmas gift of more than $2000 from many scattered friends took his breath away. Until his death it would be known as "the great present of 1867." Thereafter Frank faced life—in its financial aspects at least—from a new perspective. His determination was rejuvenated, but his hopes of continuing as the minister in Dover were soon dashed. Not being able to raise $1,000—not to mention $1,500—the society accepted Abbot's resignation. "So I am absolutely adrift," he wrote to fellow radical William J. Potter, "no pupils, no engagement anywhere, only a very faint prospect of some preaching at North Cambridge." Adversity, however, seemed only to sharpen his radicalism.

In another letter to Potter, Abbot described a lecture he gave in January of 1868, entitled "Persons and Ideas," as "the clearest and straightest statement of the essence of radicalism I have yet been able to make."[18] In March he took a final step and requested the American Unitarian Association to strike his name from its list of ministers. He

---

[17]FEA to Potter, 10 December 1867.

[18]Ibid., 16 January 1868.

then made plans for bringing his family to Cambridge, but he did not relax his message for Dover churchgoers during his final month. He spoke of the Christian "perversion" of true theism and defended his leaving the Unitarian fold.

> In resigning the names, Unitarian and Christian, I do so with full knowledge of the grave, practical consequences that must come; but wishing ever to be docile to the teachings of life, this step seems to me the plain lesson of recent circumstances. Outside of Xty must my protest against error and sin henceforth be heard; but not outside of religion, not, I trust, outside of spriritual fidelity,—not, I believe in my soul, outside of God. Face to face with Him at every step, let us toil faithfully on—you in the ancient fold, I in the broad and trackless wilderness of the outer world,—both, I pray, under the arched embrace of a still benignant Heaven.[19]

After this manifesto, the statement of Abbot's views and apology for his actions that made up his farewell sermon at the end of the month came almost as an anticlimax.

Farewell to the Unitarian Society did not mean good-bye to Dover for the Abbots. On the day of Frank's final sermon, 15 March 1868, one ardent Dover radical began organizing a movement to retain Abbot's services. Within a few days forty-five signers to a special subscription raised $1,200 for the new cause.

Despite the vexation of conservatives and the unsettled conditions, Abbot was exultant. He made perfectly clear, nonetheless, that he wanted either the old society as a whole to abandon Unitarianism and remunerate those who objected or the new liberal group to incorporate itself separately as an independent religious society. "Any intermediate course," Abbot wrote, "seems to me deficient in frankness, earnestness, and moral courage. . . . Whatever is done, let it be done boldly, justly, and kindly."[20]

Consequently the "independents" ignored the first adjourned annual meeting of the parish. As a result of their absence a motion was passed calling for the next minister to be a "Unitarian Christian." Whereupon the three church wardens (all of them supporters of Abbot), who had been elected at the regular annual meeting of 30 March,

---

[19]Dover *Gazette,* 20 March 1868. The sermon (no. 138 in his manuscript file) was delivered on 15 March 1868.

[20]Abbot to C. H. Horsch, 10 April 1868. Horsch was one of the wardens who continued to support Abbot.

resigned. Since attempts to elect new wardens failed, the annual meeting was postponed a second time.

In the meantime the radicals loosely organized the new Locust Street Independent Society. On 26 April Abbot, as the newly installed minister of this society, addressed an enthusiastic audience in American Hall, the recently dedicated city hall. In his opening address to the Dover Society entitled "New Wine in Old Bottles," Abbot optimistically announced,

> The movement which has resulted in our meeting here tonight as an Independent Society, comes, as I am most profoundly persuaded, out of no mean spite, no contemptible wrangling, no common or vulgar dissension about petty trifles in the administration of affairs. . . . I should scorn to be a party in any parish quarrel. . . . But because I believe that simply fidelity to freedom has brought us both here tonight, I rejoice in our gathering as one of the most significant events of the times. . . . It prophesies the coming day, the dawning of a better religion than that which now usurps the name. To me your movement, wholly spontaneous as it was, appears the most distinct, emphatic, unmistakable protest yet uttered against Christian superstition—the most frank and unconditioned enlistment yet made in the great cause of spiritual freedom. . . . It requires no prophet's eye, but only a wise reading of effects in their causes, to enable us to foresee the profound influence which our enterprise, if well sustained, must ultimately wield. . . . Born of the living present, we are heirs of the mighty future . . . I do in my soul believe that tonight our "American Hall" foreshadows the American Church, the church of Humanity, the Church of the People, which shall have no end but the elevation, education, and benediction of all mankind.[21]

Perhaps it was the large turnout that gave the radicals a sense of power and led them to attend the second adjourned annual meeting of the Unitarian Society scheduled for the following evening. In any event, the radicals were in a majority, and even through the formal notations of the parish minutes one can perceive the rancor and suspicion that such a circumstance aroused. The nominating committee had put forward three well-known conservatives; Samuel Hale's motion that all ballots must be signed was carried; and one member from each faction was appointed to count ballots. The count, to the conservatives' dismay, revealed that by a vote of 53 to 48 the three radicals who had previously resigned had been reelected.

---

[21]"New Wine in Old Bottles," opening address to the First Independent Society of Dover, New Hampshire, 26 April 1868. Manuscript Sermon file.

Then came the real coup: Samuel Wheeler (an acute lawyer who, Abbot would later say, was secretly hostile to the new enterprise), without recognizing the existence of an independent society, moved that "each of the two divisions of said Society be entitled to the use of the Meeting House one half of the time." This motion was then passed by virtually the same margin (53 to 46). It thus appeared that the "friends of Mr. Abbot" had won a great victory, and it is no wonder that the *Gazette,* in reporting the election of this committee, should have added that "the new church . . . sets forth in its journey through life under the most favorable auspices." Abbot was elated by the enthusiasm for his doctrines and not displeased, it would seem, by the arrangements that were made.[22]

But all was not well. Benjamin Barnes, who had crossed swords with Abbot back in 1865, now organized a counterattack. On 21 and 23 May Barnes presented to the wardens two protests challenging the legality of the arrangement. Both were signed first by Barnes, one being from "members" of the society, with eighty-six names, the other from "pew holders," with forty-three names. On 10 June the radical group was served notice that on or before 16 June the subscribers would seek an injunction from the Supreme Judicial Court of New Hampshire.

Not until news of this "protest" had been bruited about did Abbot investigate and in so doing discover that the motion conveying rights to the radical group was worded to imply that he was still preaching to the liberal wing of a Unitarian Church and not to an independent group at all. To set this matter right morally and to counter the action of Barnes, Abbot had to induce the radicals to organize themselves more formally. To this end Abbot and the radicals met on 9 June, elected three men as wardens and named a committee to consider a constitution that would document their existence as an "Independent Religious Society." To this committee Abbot submitted "Articles of Agreement," which stated that the purposes of the society "shall be to uphold the principles of free religion in this community by whatever methods it shall deem proper, and to advance the cause of truth, righteousness, and love, throughout the world." The actions expected to follow from this meeting, however, were never taken. Abbot's Articles were not acted upon and no further legal business meetings were held.

---

[22]Dover *Gazette,* 22 May 1868; Parish Records, 27 April 1868.

Now Abbot and his followers had reached a dilemma. Their opponents had approved the use of the meetinghouse for both divisions of the society. If the Independents organized a separate society, the motion at the annual meeting would be rendered void and the church building would be lost to them. If the Independents did not organize a separate society, they would have to continue being Unitarians. This dilemma led to the celebrated legal case *Hale vs. Everett*.

Since Abbot was trying to force his supporters to take a strong, unequivocal stand that would not "sacrifice principle to policy," the conservatives, led by Samuel Hale and Benjamin Barnes, Jr., laid their case before the Supreme Judicial Court of New Hampshire during the June term. The defendants, including all the members of the "Independent Society" and Abbot, were on 9 June given notice that a bill in chancery was being filed and that while this bill was pending, the plaintiffs would apply for a temporary injunction to the First Judicial District Court, to be held at Exeter.

Samuel Hale also indicated privately that efforts would be made to indict Abbot himself under a New Hampshire statute that made it illegal for a person "openly [to] deny the being of God, or wilfully blaspheme the name of God, Jesus Christ, or the Holy Ghost, or [to] . . . curse or reproach the word of God contained in the canonical books of the old and new testaments." Action in this direction, however, was not taken since the main purpose of the legal action was accomplished long before a decision was reached or a decree issued.[23]

The bill (in equity) filed by the plaintiffs was a detailed résumé of the history of the First Unitarian Society of Christians in Dover from its preorganizational period to the present. The immediate concern of the case was the control of the meetinghouse. The conservatives stressed that under each of its ministers the society had taught and inculcated the doctrines of Christianity "as holden by that sect of Christians called Unitarian." Abbot and his supporters, the conservatives maintained, had departed from this tradition, depriving "these plaintiffs of their right to hear Christianity preached in the church."[24]

The defendants (excepting Abbot) answered by insisting that their action was legally taken and that the plaintiffs still were allowed to

---

[23]James W. Bartlett to FEA, 28 July 1868; cited in *The General Statutes of the State of New Hampshire*, 255, §1, 514.

[24]The fullest account of *Hale vs. Everett* are the reprints of the trial reports, "Samuel Hale & als. *versus* Charles Z. Everett & als.," *Reprints of Cases Argued and Determined in the Supreme Judicial Court of New Hampshire* (John M. Shirley, state reporter).

use the church. Abbot, in his own "answer" to the bill, merely stated that Wallingford, Everett, and Folsom (indicating that they spoke as duly delegated authorities) asked him to be their preacher for one year, and on Sabbaths he had done that to the best of his ability.

Involved in the case was the question of the nature of Unitarianism. The founders, the conservatives continued, organized a society of "Unitarian *Christians*," under a statute of New Hampshire law that conferred privileges of organization only to Christians. In accordance with Congregational polity and notwithstanding later actions of the Unitarian Conference, the Dover Society gave its approval to the doctrine of the "Messiahship of Christ." Extensive depositions proved that the founders were substantially at one with the present conservatives in the case. Abbot, on the contrary, had explicitly taken a position outside of Unitarianism and Christianity and was preaching to an independent religious society. This was an undesirable situation. "Christ and Anti-Christ being in nature and spirit antagonistical," it was argued that these differing views could not be preached in the same meetinghouse without subverting the foundations of the society. The membership, moreover, had voted overwhelmingly that their next minister should be a "Unitarian Christian."

The radicals, however, countered by claiming that the society was duly incorporated under the laws of the state, which did *not* limit such organization to Christians. By agreement of the founders the "general custody of the house" was placed under the control of the society. Referring to the articles of association as well, the radicals emphasized the provision that the church was to be devoted to the "publick worship of God." The word *Christian,* they said, appeared only in the *name* of the society. Furthermore, in an adjourned annual meeting, the divided use of the building had been duly approved and this agreement had been abided by, with the result that the other division had the building for as much time as had been felt necessary in the past ten years. The existence of an independent religious society was denied.

It was not true, the radicals averred, that Unitarianism was being distorted, for that sect had contained persons of all varieties of opinion, and in the National Unitarian Conference of 1868 it had been overwhelmingly voted that not even the confessional statements of their own constitution were to be considered binding. As for Abbot himself, he was not an infidel nor had he deified reason; he worshipped God devoutly and humbly. Granting an injunction, therefore, would be an infringement of freedom of religion. The radicals made a case that the specific mention of Abbot by name ruled out the possibility of his conversion to conservative principles.

Clarity was not one of the attributes of the 266 pages of the "Dover Case." The recent history of the society and the allegedly nonexistent independent society were so snarled, the problem of membership so confusing, and the entire matter so submerged in theological disputation that the briefs no less than the opinions constantly threatened to hide the real issue completely. Fundamentally, however, the question was this: were the wardens of the society authorized by the terms under which the society had been founded to allow the meetinghouse to be used by an independent religious group that hired a minister who was an outspoken critic of Christianity?

Not until December did the court issue its ruling. In the meantime the justices were busy studying theology and the history of religion in America. It was said that Justice Charles Doe spent six months in research on these subjects before writing his dissent. In 1875 when the official report was finally published, the *American Law Review* remarked that "the case will be a very mine of learning to the student [of law, history, and theology] and the practising lawyer." Associate Justice J. Everett Sargent spoke for the court, with Associate Justice Charles Doe dissenting. The wardens and members of the radical factions were enjoined from hiring Abbot or anyone with like views, and the present wardens or any other wardens or members were forbidden to employ as preacher anyone who held doctrines "subversive of the fundamental doctrines of the denomination of Christians known as Unitarians." The opinion of Justice Sargent was an eighty-page document. In a series of long introductory arguments, Justice Sargent made clear that the court had not ruled on the basis of any statutory limitation on religious freedom. He then entered into more theological matters and an examination of the facts of the Dover troubles. The decision came to rest essentially on two propositions.

First, that for forty years the Dover Society had continued in the spirit of the founders as a "Unitarian Christian" organization, whereas "Deists, theists, free religionists, and other infidels, though they may be Unitarians in some sense are not Unitarian Christians" (12 and 76).[25] Support of this proposition was adduced by reference to the views of prominent early Unitarians and ministers of the society, and by consideration of certain affirmations Abbot made at his ordination (93). Congregational polity notwithstanding, "to find what are the re-

---

[25]These page references are to *Hale vs. Everett* trial reports.

ligious opinions of a Congregational society, we must look at the creed, or confession, or doctrines of the church with which it is connected" (12). A name such as "Unitarian Christian" was held to be per se a creed (92).

Second, "if a meeting-house is conveyed . . . to be under the control of a society of Christians, it would be the duty of the court . . . to see that the house was controlled by a society of Christians." This position is in turn based on the proposition that if a division in the parish occurs, it is necessary to determine whether or not one group "seceded from the doctrines and faith of the original sect" (77). If so, it was ruled that "members who secede from a church or religious society thereby forfeit all right to any part of the property, rights, or privileges of such church and society" (12). Using such a theory it was not difficult to produce factual support. On the doctrinal level Abbot had clearly and repeatedly, both publicly and privately, taken a position outside Christianity. "The soul is its own Christ. Humanity is its own Messiah," he was quoted as having said (89). That many Unitarians took positions parallel in many points to Abbot's merely indicated that "many Unitarians are not Christians" (91). In this light, Abbot's status as in some vague sense a "Protestant" (since he was non- or anti-Catholic) was held to be irrelevant. On the organizational level Sargent found that the Independents had clearly organized themselves separately as a secessionist group even if legal incorporation had not been accomplished (102).

It is important to realize, however, that the frequent charges that Justice Sargent's decision was a bigoted, obscurantist, or "evangelical" one are not true. Sargent emphatically affirmed the right of people to hold to heterodox opinions of any sort (9 and 77) and he decried the existence of religious qualifications in New Hampshire's constitutions and statutes. Despite his own orthodox views, Sargent expressed the greatest esteem for Abbot's personal integrity and chided the defendants who would "compromise their own consistency and integrity, for the sake of success in a paltry suit at law" (106). In a technical sense, one shortcoming of Sargent's opinion was its failure to meet the argument of Judge Doe regarding the proper action to be taken against seceders or trespassers. But the most serious criticisms of the opinion were that it was legalistic in the extreme, leaving historical and social considerations out of mind, and it failed to show the sensitivity to particular circumstances expected in the exercise of chancery jurisdiction. The result was a decision that had virtually no applicability to the contemporary situation, and which, if taken lit-

erally, would have disrupted nearly every congregationally organized church in the state.

The dissent of Judge Doe, on the other hand, was up-to-date and
practical, a forceful opinion by an interesting judge, but hardly distinguished for its logic. Born in 1830, he was a graduate of Dartmouth
and a recipient of a term's legal training at the Harvard Law School.
In 1859 Charles Doe was appointed to the supreme New Hampshire
bench at the age of twenty-nine. Although removed from the bench
in 1874, when the Democrats came to power in the state, he was reap-
pointed as chief justice in 1876 when the Republicans gained office,
and served until 1896. Charles Doe is, according to Roscoe Pound,
"one of the ten best judges in American judicial history."[26] His recognition of the social nature of law and its historical mutability en-
deared him to Pound; and if his insistent defense of the rights of
property identifies him with nineteenth-century American jurispru-
dence, then his constant protection of civil liberties places him in the
tradition of Oliver Wendell Holmes. The Dover Case demonstrated
that when property rights and civil rights conflicted (or seemed to
conflict) Doe would take his stand for the latter.

His dissent was in large part a spirited defense of religious freedom and an eloquent affirmation of Abbot's right to believe as he
chose. Neither of these pleas was directly related to the issue, however, for Judge Sargent had likewise insisted that both the state and
national constitutions made these guarantees. Yet Doe did not fail to
make specific replies to Sargent's two central contentions. As for the
claim that the *name* designated the platform or creed of the society,
Doe ridiculed the idea, saying that the name *Unitarian* no more bound
members to theological doctrines than the name of the town, *Jackson,*
limited its citizens to the platform of the Democratic party (232). He
pointed out that the chief purpose of the founders had been to provide
for the "publick worship of God." He also found that neither the incorporating charter nor the authorizing law made any confessional
limitation.

With regard to the second point—that the creed designated was a
specific system of biblical Christianity—Doe insisted that the cardinal point of the founders was being ignored: "They were intelligent
men. They were theologically liberal, in the large Unitarian sense"

---

[26]Roscoe Pound, *The Formative Era of American Law;* cited in "Doe of
New Hampshire: Reflections on a Nineteenth-Century Judge," *Harvard Law
Review* 63 (1950): 513.

(258). Operating in a congregational pattern that was free in the first place, they gave it a still larger freedom; they were in revolt from creeds and dogmatics (257). It is the plaintiffs, Doe said, who have abandoned the spirit of Channing (273). Doe charged that it was not a duty of the court to insure the unchangeableness of 1827 Unitarianism. Nor, he said, should the court ignore the development of religion in New England by failing to recognize that six of the eight Unitarian churches in the state in 1827 "had apostasized from orthodoxy" themselves (268). According to this decree, he argued, one irate reactionary could call a whole liberal Congregational parish back to the theology of Jonathan Edwards!

In retrospect, though one can see how contemporaries misgauged the significance of the case, it is still very difficult to estimate the influence of the Dover troubles on Unitarian history. One thing is reasonably clear: the Dover controversy was not a key in the struggle for civil liberties. Civil liberties were never challenged and, in addition, the judge who spoke for the court revealed a deep concern for such rights. On this question Abbot himself vacillated. On the very day the injunction was granted, he took little comfort in the "very radical and very manly" dissenting opinion of Judge Doe. Abbot was unconvinced that radicalism could ever flourish in the Unitarian church, and this made him regard the practical implications of the decision as "exceedingly important": "In this state, at least, it makes a very great difference whether a radical calls himself a Christian or not; for no Unitarian Society is now permitted by law to employ a non-Christian as its minister, neither is an unsectarian minister permitted to perform the marriage service."[27]

What was the effect of the Dover case? There is some evidence that the decision did strengthen the conservative cause, and in several later cases Unitarian societies were able to eject radical ministers or factions on similar grounds. But the technical complexities of the Dover situation and the sense of unreality pervading Sargent's opinion, together with the idealistic and pragmatic appeal of Doe's dissent, limited the case's importance as a legal precedent. In the long run, it seems that such judicial support as the case provided for conservatism was probably cancelled by the opprobrium attached to such deliberate resistance to congregational desires.

The case nevertheless dramatized the internal rift in Unitarian thought by laying bare the intrinsic tension between the "liberalism"

---

[27]FEA to Potter, 16 December 1868.

and the "Christianity" of the denomination. The court's decision made obvious the immense difficulty of maintaining a position that sought at least verbally to establish the authority of reason within an evangelical framework. Finally, the case steeled the will and intensified the determination of Francis Abbot, who went on to defy official Unitarianism by inducing a society in Toledo to leave the National Conference and by founding in that city the *Index,* a journal of Free Religion that for a decade waged a running battle with all forms of Christianity.

This, however, had little effect on the immediate case at hand since Abbot had much earlier resigned over the failure of the radicals to sever all connections from the Unitarian Society by legally incorporating themselves. Hence, once again, in October 1868 Abbot found himself unemployed and isolated. Yet his days as a minister were not over, nor was he to be faced with the abhorrent task of drilling delinquent students. Abbot's reputation as a courageous "liberal" had traveled far, and a society in Toledo wanted him as its minister—or to hear him at least. "That I have accomplished so little here, after all, extinguishes what little vanity I had concerning my service," he had confessed to Potter. "The lesson to myself is a needed one, perhaps, however severe: henceforth let me work more humbly and self-forgettingly. I take my failure as a deserved rebuke, and mean to profit by it." One could wonder if he would demonstrate an understanding of Dover's lessons in Toledo.[28]

---

[28]Ibid., 19 October 1868.

CHAPTER FIVE

THE DEFECTION OF THE RADICALS

BECAUSE THE LIBERAL FAITH of New England flourished on the native ground of a congregational polity that encouraged doctrinal variation, it was perhaps inevitable that the Transcendental revolt would lead to the formation of a radical faction within the Unitarian movement itself. These radicals represented an ancient tradition that Emerson, by the beauty of his words, or Parker by the energy of his activities, merely reemphasized in American terms. Some of them took their inspiration from the long Socinian (in contrast to Arian) tradition and placed their emphasis on a humanitarian Christology. Many of these radicals turned to the idealistic philosophy that had been given such magnificent expression by the post-Kantian philosophers of Germany. Others placed their faith in science, championing the new views that arose first in geology and then in biology, and translating both into a fervently optimistic developmental interpretation of humanity's social and spiritual experience. Virtually all of them met with secularists, statesmen, and reformers on common ground and expressed their religious impulses increasingly in the categories of moralism. Almost without exception they regarded Channing as they regarded Luther, as a transitional hero in the progressive evolution of pure and absolute religion.

The degree of radicalism naturally varied from individual to individual, and at times it was incongruously combined with conservatism; but because even the milder men possessed the enthusiasm that usually accompanies the advocacy of change, the conservatives were alarmed by the apparent increase of this party of infidelity.

Ever since Andrews Norton's famous diatribe on the "Latest Form of Infidelity" (1839), the parties had been fairly clearly defined, and even as the Civil War went into its final bloody year the radicals had failed to gain any important hold on the educational institutions or other organizations of the denomination. Because of the exceedingly loose organization of Unitarianism, however, the danger of this development was recognized by many. Because they realized as well that much of the early élan of the movement had been lost since its position on the American religious scene had become fairly secure, it was widely felt that concerted action should be taken not only to revitalize Unitarianism but to organize it more effectively.

There were at the time ten organizations that could be termed in some sense official. Three of these were state federations of Unitarian churches in Maine, New Hampshire, and New York. The Conference of Western Unitarian Churches (established in 1852) was similar though much less coordinated and more widely flung. Three organizations were essentially educational: the Society for Promoting Theological Education, which had been organized in 1816 for the purpose of subsidizing the Harvard Divinity School and its students; Meadville Theological School, which though nondenominational was opened under Unitarian auspices in 1844 to provide ministers for the West; and Antioch College, Ohio, where for a time the Unitarians and the anti-Calvinistic Christian Connection cooperated.

There were three essentially missionary organizations: the Massachusetts Evangelical Mission Society (the oldest of all, having been instituted in 1807), the Sunday School Society (founded in 1827), and the most influential organization, the American Unitarian Association. The A.U.A. was the most widely representative organization of the denomination. Its publications made Unitarianism known to America; its offices coordinated mission activities; and it kept a registry of pastors and performed innumerable other executive functions. Although membership depended only on the payment of a one-dollar-annual or a thirty-dollar-lifetime fee, the A.U.A. exercised great influence.

After the Unitarians had been more or less accepted into the New England religious community, these several organizations began to languish. In its report for May 1864, the A.U.A. announced that no more than fifty churches (representing only one-sixth of the Unitarian membership) were supporting its diverse activities, thus reducing its budget during the preceding year to $6,800.[1] Under these circumstances a special meeting of the membership was summoned to consider an ingathering of $25,000. At this important meeting, which was held in the Hollis Street Church, Boston, on 6-7 December 1864, the members not only approved the campaign but voted unanimously to raise the goal to $100,000. Rufus P. Stebbins, president of the A.U.A., was made chairman of the Finance Committee. The general purpose

---

[1]*Report of the [First] Convention of Unitarian Churches Held in New York on the 5th and 6th of April, 1865* (Boston, 1886) ii-xi (hereafter *1865 Report*).

of this fund was "to aid in the spread and establishment of the truth as it is in Jesus," but missionary aid, work in the Federal armies, and agents in the new territory "won from rebellion" were the special activities planned for within this broad aim.[2]

Of much greater significance for the future of Unitarianism was the resolution of Henry W. Bellows, the famous minister of the Church of All Souls in New York, which carried at this convention: "That a committee of ten persons, three ministers and seven laymen, be appointed to call a convention to consist of the pastor and two delegates from each church or parish in the Unitarian denomination, to meet in the city of New York, to consider the interests of our cause, and to institute measures for its good." Bellows was no mean opponent for the radical party. As the originator, organizer, and president of the United States Sanitary Commission during the Civil War, Bellows was probably one of the most powerful and respected of the Unitarian clergy.

Bellows's resolution, however, was far from being the reactionary action that Abbot and the radicals perceived. It rather reflected a new spirit within Unitarianism that had been slowly germinating for a decade. Beginning in the mid-1850s a position had developed among some Unitarians that placed far more emphasis than previously on the church as an institution.[3] This party, which included among its devotees not only Bellows but also Frederic Henry Hedge and James Freeman Clarke, identified its position as "Broad Church." This term was originally used to describe those Anglicans who attempted to transcend the High Church/Low Church division within the Church of England. "Broad Church" Unitarians likewise attempted to supersede the divisions within their denomination. They willingly accepted much of the intuitionalism of the Transcendentalists, but they

---

[2]From the notice published by the Executive Committee of the A.U.A. immediately after the meeting.

[3]This "middle party" has been an important area of study among recent historians. See, in particular, Conrad Wright, *The Liberal Christians: Essays on American Unitarian History* (Boston: Beacon Press, 1970) 81-109; Conrad Wright, ed., *A Stream of Light: A Sesquicentennial History of American Unitarianism* (Boston: Unitarian Universalist Association, 1975); and David Robinson, *The Unitarians and the Universalists* (Westport CT: Greenwood Press, 1985). Perhaps the most important enunciation of this impulse was Bellows's sermon, "The Suspense of Faith," delivered to the alumni of Harvard Divinity School on 19 July 1859. On Bellows, see Walter Donald Kring, *Henry Whitney Bellows* (Boston: Skinner House, 1979).

emphasized the importance of the church as a comprehensive institution. Furthermore they argued that any growth of ecclesiastical self-
consciousness had to recognize the Christian elements that were part
of the historic definition of Unitarianism. It was on this issue that the
radicals chafed.

Abbot and some of his friends had been well aware that this meeting could be put to conservative uses and they tried to muster a good
representation of the liberal-radical group for the occasion, but without avail. In all respects they were ignored or outvoted and their opponents dominated the new committees. The "Call" to the Convention
of Unitarian churches appeared on 1 February, to be followed by an
"Address to the Churches" written by the three clerical members of
the committee. The latter was an unambiguously Christian document
that served as the opening salvo of the great struggle for control of the
future of Unitarianism.

On the eve of the convention (4 April 1865), with the $100,000
all but subscribed, the delegates gathered in All Souls Church, New
York. There they heard a sermon by James Freeman Clarke, the famous Christian Transcendentalist. Speaking on a favorite missionary
text, Clarke encouraged them to take up boldly the task before them,
but to do it as Christians. He spoke a word for freedom: "I often find
myself in the fullest Christian sympathy with those from whom I most
widely differ in theology." Still, it was a Christian sermon.

> So, while Love is the only thing needful as the end, Faith is the only
> thing needful as the means. . . . The saving, essential faith is not the
> belief in any doctrines about Christ, but is trusting in Christ himself.
> It is putting our hand in his, to be led by him. . . . It is part of our mis-
> sion to the nineteenth century to show the heresy of putting anything
> between Christ and those he is to save. . . . Are we Unitarians be-
> cause we like being shut out from the sympathy of the Church? No.
> We often long for the larger communion of the universal Church. . . .
> The great body of Unitarians are not philosophers, but Christians; the
> great heart of our body beats with warm love for the Savior.[4]

The delegates assembled on the following morning and "the program moved with the smoothness of a well-oiled machine." Bellows
had been quoted by one of the radicals as having privately said before
the meeting, "I don't know as we can manage it, but if we could some
way contrive to slough off some of this radical element, it would be a

---

[4]*1865 Report*, 3-32.

great thing for our denomination."[5] In essentials Bellows was successful in this resolve. Much of the business was prepared beforehand
by the Committee on Arrangements. Less than an hour was required
to open the meeting and elect the officers. By means of a Committee
on the Order of Business, which in turn proposed that a Committee
on Organization report proposals on constitutional matters, and by
timely speeches from the floor, every liberal assault on the prear-
ranged business was either tabled, referred, or defeated.

After a minimum of debate the following resolution was passed:

> *Preamble.—Whereas,* The great opportunities and demands for
> Christian labor and consecration at this time increase our sense of the
> obligations of all disciples of the Lord Jesus Christ to prove their faith
> by self-denial, and by the devotion of their lives and possessions to
> the Service of God and the building-up of the kingdom of his Son,—
>
> *Article I.*—Therefore, the Christian churches of the Unitarian faith
> here assembled unite themselves in a common body, to be known as the
> National Conference of Unitarian Churches, to the end of energizing and
> stimulating the denomination with which they are connected to the larg-
> est exertions in the cause of Christian faith and work.[6]

Unitarianism was, in the eyes of many radicals, committed to what
was substantially a confessional statement.

With this major business taken care of, other practical and pro-
pagandistic matters were taken up. The body passed six resolutions
for expanded action: that the A.U.A. $100,000 fund be subscribed for
this year and annually thereafter; that another $100,000 be raised for
Antioch College; that the Executive Council create an organ of the
denomination to be called the *Liberal Christian;* and that the theological schools and the Western Conference be generously supported.
Thereafter officers were elected and the convention was adjourned.

From the perspective of the radicals, the convention was unques-
tionably a conservative victory: the articles of faith were imbedded
in the constitution and conservatives dominated the Executive Council, which was, in turn, entrusted with founding an organ of opinion.

---

[5]J. L. Hatch to FEA, 22 November 1866. For a description of the con-
vention from the radicals' perspective, see Stow Persons, *Free Religion* (New
Haven: Yale University Press, 1948) 15ff. For a very different account, see
Conrad Wright, *The Liberal Christians,* 81-109.

[6]*1865 Report,* 46-47. An even more conservative pronouncement that
professed belief in miracles, the resurrection of the dead, and other points of
doctrine was also set forward, but it was too evangelical even for Bellows.

The only consolation that the liberals could derive from the proceedings was the general resolution that had been passed.

> *Resolved,* That to secure the largest Unity of the Spirit, and the widest practical co-operation of our Body, it is hereby understood that all the resolutions and declarations of this Convention are expressions only of its majority, committing in no degree those who object to them, claiming no other than a moral authority over the members of the Convention, or the Churches represented here, and are all dependent wholly for their effect upon the consent they command on their own merits, from the Churches here represented or belonging within the circle of our special fellowship.[7]

Yet, the importance of such a resolution for the radicals (in the light of the seemingly contradictory provisions in the organic law of the conference) was, at best, debatable.

Abbot had not taken part in the meeting itself and therefore the one dissenting vote on the preamble was not his; but he increasingly began to believe that the new Unitarian "confederation" had been founded on principles that placed grievous limitations on the movement's freedom and future. With the passing months Abbot came more and more to regard those enactments (particularly the preamble) as a blight on the denomination, a limitation of his own freedom, and the enshrinement of a great theological error.

His radicalism gradually came to dominate his sermons. Lectures, agitation, and an immense correspondence left less and less time for "pastoral care." By the following July he had taken a firm position: "I have made my resolve, and mean to fight it out on the radical line if it takes me all eternity. There are enough [persons] to build *societies.*"[8] From this time on Abbot concentrated on the approaching second convention of the National Conference, to be held in the Church of the Messiah in Syracuse in October (1866). It remains to consider the nature and effects of his larger crusade. When Abbot left Dover for Syracuse he was prepared to put up a strong battle for complete religious freedom.

Arriving on the eve of the convention, he conferred with Edward Everett Hale and made known his intention of bringing up the matter. Hale stated that the debate was scheduled for the second day. On the "bright October day" when the body first assembled for business, however, any chance for avoiding the issue had been prevented by

---

[7]Ibid., 39.

[8]FEA to Anne Mumford, 30 July 1866.

Abbot's having his proposed revision of the preamble and first article printed and placed in the pews beforehand. No one could call them evasive.

> *Whereas* the object of Christianity is the universal diffusion of Love, Righteousness, and Truth; and the attainment of this object depends, under God, upon individual and collective Christian activity: and collective Christian activity, to be efficient, must be thoroughly organized; and
>
> *Whereas* perfect freedom of thought, which is at once the right and duty of every human being, always leads to diversity of opinion, and is therefore hindered by common creeds or statements of faith; and
>
> *Whereas* the only reconciliation of the duties of collective Christian activity and individual freedom of thought, lies in an efficient organization for practical Christian work, based rather on unity of spirit than on uniformity of belief:
>
> *Article I.*—Therefore the Churches here assembled, disregarding all sectarian or theological differences, and offering a cordial fellowship to all who will join with them in Christian work, unite themselves in a common body to be known as *The National Conference of Unitarian and Independent Churches.*[9]

After hearing and approving the reports, and the election of a panel of officers, which was headed by the Honorable Thomas D. Eliot as president, the panel was seen to be as conservative in makeup as the preceding year's roster. Abbot addressed the assembly on behalf of his proposed revision, and on the motion of Frederic H. Hedge the convention voted to take up Abbot's resolution that very afternoon. The chances for acceptance, of course, were extremely slim. The opposition to Abbot's resolution was perhaps most succinctly stated by Bellows himself: "The good sense of the Unitarian denomination had discerned that it must either submit to turn into a small philosophical sect, or else perform the duties of a Christian Church, which recognizes the world as its field."[10] Bellows was also very active during the recess between 1:00 and 3:00 P.M., and he succeeded in lining up a heavy array of speakers, as many as possible of them younger men, to oppose Abbot's revision. The outcome of the conflict was clear from the start, and Abbot's revision was decisively defeated. Furthermore, the convention passed an amendment from James Freeman Clarke

---

[9]*Free Church Tracts No. 9,* 14ff.; *1865 Report,* 20.

[10]*1865 Report,* 4.

stating that "other Christian Churches" were made eligible to join the conference.[11]

The real nature of the debates that finally ended in the defeat of Abbot's revision and the adoption of this other amendment is suggested more accurately in the fact that Abbot's attempts even to liberalize the *interpretation* of the amendment were foiled by the oratory of A. D. Mayo, of Cincinnati, and by the sheer weight of conservative and Broad Church numbers. Another radical, J. L. Hatch, on the second afternoon of the convention proposed another resolution designed to liberalize Clarke's amendment. Hatch would affirm that "we do not mean to exclude religious societies which have no distinctive church organization, and are not nominally Christian, if they desire to cooperate with us in what we call Christian work."[12] This action was merely referred to the Committee on Business for burial. Hatch was furious, and he went home accusing both Bellows and Clarke of having acted in bad faith ever since the meetings of 1864. Hatch insisted to Abbot later that "the principle involved was the same, and . . . the Conference by their rejection of my resolution, under the circumstances, clearly refused to reaffirm and apply the principle of complete doctrinal freedom of its members resolved on at New York with the express cooperation of our body."[13] The official report of Hatch's resolution and the action taken on it deliberately omitted any of the discussion and suggested that the matter was handled virtually without discussion or disagreement. Abbot revealed that such was not the case.

The rest of the convention was devoted to affairs relating to the expanded work of the conference. Bellows reported more than $250,000 subscribed for Antioch, success on the first $100,000 drive for the A.U.A. and more than $60,000 collected on the second, and a decision to strengthen both the *Christian Register* and the *Christian Inquirer* rather than start a new periodical. There were also many reports and addresses stressing the need for new pastors and wider mission work in America, especially in the West. Drives for another $100,000 for the A.U.A. and $35,000 for the Meadville Theological School were approved; multifarious other projects were discussed or inaugurated. It must be remembered that whatever the radicals would have said about exclusion, it was a fact that organization and lead-

---

[11]Ibid., 21.

[12]Ibid., 44-45.

[13]Hatch to FEA, 8 April 1867.

ership had revitalized Unitarianism in America, creating essentially a denominational awakening.

To the defeated radicals, the prospect did not seem so auspicious. "I never went to bed a sadder man," wrote Abbot. To these men, the Syracuse Convention was a painful demonstration of Christian authority. Soon after their return, moreover, the conflict broke into the open as radicals were literally excluded by the various regional conferences that affirmed the preamble. The threat of this kind of action polarized Abbot's outlook. "I am fairly launched into a conflict to which I can see no end. A revolution in the denomination is approaching, and I must be in the thickest of it. . . . Sacrifices must be made by all of us, but I care not; I have pledged to this cause all that I have and am, and may God prosper the truth!"[14] After this decision the minister of Dover's quiet church became a propagandist and organizer of radicalism.

The "Battle of Syracuse" was thus a defeat for the radicals; and with exclusion facing them, these embittered opponents of the preamble resolved to take action. The murmurs of discontent that had been heard since 1865 grew to a chorus as the more ardent among the "excluded" began reflecting on their plight. Discussions had followed the adverse vote in Syracuse. William J. Potter—who began his religious life as a Quaker only to be touched by Transcendentalism, and who finally became Abbot's closest friend and Free Religion's most devoted servant—tells of his own vision "in the night-watches before leaving Syracuse . . . of a spiritual anti-slavery Society . . . with the larger object of liberating religion from every sort of thraldom to irrational and merely traditional authority."[15]

The initial action seems to have been taken by the most impetuous of all the excluded radicals, Edward C. Towne, who was then minister in Medford. Towne visited the Reverend C. A. Bartol of West Church in Boston (who, if not a radical, was suspicious of narrow denominationalism) almost immediately upon his return and found him willing to begin action even though he had not been present at the convention.

> He feels [wrote Towne] that there is no alternative now but for a new organization. . . . I go for the immediate organization of the American

---

[14]FEA to Anne Mumford, 10 December 1866.

[15]William J. Potter, *The Free Religious Association: Its Twenty-Five Years and Their Meaning* (Boston, 1892) 9 (hereafter *Historical Address*).

Liberal Conference, or something of that sort. We can make a pro-
visional organization this winter at a meeting in Boston, and prepare
for a full meeting next October when the National does not meet. What
do you say?[16]

In response to this parley, Bartol issued an informal call for a meeting
of radicals in his home. On the appointed day nine men gathered in a
semicircle around the blazing hearth in Dr. Bartol's parlor. The
younger, more fervent men were in the center and their elderly host
was near the fire. Samuel Johnson, the student of Oriental religions,
and John Weiss, the biographer of Theodore Parker, were the
spokesmen for individualism and freedom, but the others urged organization of some sort.[17]

A second informal meeting was scheduled, and for this Abbot made
more positive preparations. He wrote to Potter a week before the
meeting analyzing the Syracuse Conference in detail and insisting that
the radicals had been formally—whether intentionally or not—excluded. Abbot also defined his organizational goals: "But, my dear sir,
we have a most high and solemn duty to discharge apart from the
Conference. We must affirm the possibility of a diviner cooperation
than that of a sect." Bartol approved of what Abbot put forward, indicating that he too was not content without some organizational "em-
bodiment" of radical principles. It was thus with these proposals before
them that the original group plus two or three additions met again on
26 November.[18]

Although further discussion revealed the same cleavage of opinion between individualists and organizationalists, it became clear that
even the individualists would not resist or impede organization. At
another informal meeting a few weeks later, the group appointed Abbot, Potter, and Towne to arrange for a more definitive and wider
meeting of radicals. Potter tells how, upon leaving Bartol's friendly
house on Chestnut Street, the three men paused on Boston Common
and before separation "took each other's hands in a mutual pledge to
stand true to the purpose which they had at heart until they should
see it accomplished."[19]

Abbot, Potter, and Towne were in complete agreement that a new
organization was necessary. Abbot advanced these views publicly in

---

[16]Towne to FEA, 14 October 1866.

[17]Potter describes this meeting in *Historical Address*.

[18]FEA to Potter, 21 November 1866; Bartol to FEA, 21 November 1866.

[19]Potter, *Historical Address,* 12.

a strongly phrased article on "Organization" in the *Radical*. His argument was based on two "axioms": that "all finite life must become organic" and that "finite life is higher in degree, the more highly organic it becomes."

> The most profoundly philosophical view of human society is that which makes the race an organism. . . . Pure individualism is the crudest type of human existence . . . the great problem of sociology is the right adjustment of the relations between the unit and the aggregate. . . . The ideal end of society is accomplished in the *highest possible development of all its individual members, according to the law of their natural individualities*. . . . This mutual existence of the individual for society, and of society for the individual, constitutes the human race as a single organism, which the immortal Kant defines as "that in which the whole and the parts are mutually means and ends."
> . . . What I have said has a plain bearing on the times. If there is any real vitality in the "radical movement," it will express itself in associate action, work out collective self-affirmation, and become an organized power. . . . I do not believe in voluntary secession or schism; but no man can prevent involuntary exclusion. . . . The radicals, therefore, find themselves at last definitively excluded from the only organization from which they could expect the affirmation of their own great principles. . . . It is time for a new organization on a new basis. It is useless to organize on intellectual finalities. . . . That is the mischief of creeds. . . . The only bond of union elastic enough to leave free play for individual growth, must be a platform *of principles that are laws of life, of purposes and ends that are life itself*. . . . It will be the affirmation of *progress* as the law of humanity.[20]

Abbot then appended for consideration a sketch of a proposed constitution, and followed up his demands with a letter on "Creeds and Unitarianism" in May and his Parker Fraternity address on "A Radical's Theology," which was published in June.[21] Nor was Abbot alone in these controversies. The great debate was carried on in all of the Unitarian periodicals, while Joseph Marvin, Henry B. Blackwell, Towne, and others continued the argument in the *Radical*.

In these hours of decision, however, Bartol decided to align himself with the individualists, Johnson and Weiss, and dissociate himself from active participation in the movement. The loss of so eminent a man as Bartol fortunately was compensated by the enlistment of an ally "whose name alone was felt to be worth a thousand men—Oc-

[20]"Organization," *The Radical* 2:4 (December 1866): 219-25.

[21]Ibid., 2:9 (May 1867): 571-73, and 2:10 (June 1867): 585-97.

tavius B. Frothingham." And it was this renowned New York preacher
who undertook to write the "Call" for the projected meeting.[22]

Abbot thought the message too indefinite and weak, but along with
Bartol, Weiss, Towne, Potter, and others he signed it, and it was dispatched on 1 January 1867. Abbot journeyed to Boston early, delivering his address to the Parker Fraternity on Sunday evening (3
February). On the following day, Towne, Potter, and he had a "little
congress" at the home of Mrs. Theodore Parker, where they drafted
a constitution. Abbot remembered later that his main contribution was
the "first sentence of article II," which made clear the complete freedom of every member. At 11:00 on the following morning, with
Frothingham in the chair, the committee rendered its report to the
twenty-five or thirty liberals who assembled. It was a diverse group
of liberal Unitarians, Universalists, and Quakers—mostly clergymen,
though a number of members from Parker's old Twenty-Eighth Congregational Society were there.

Agreeing on the general principle that membership would not
constitute or require a formal break with Unitarianism, the group accepted the proposed constitution. Then they appointed a committee
to plan a large public meeting in late May for the purposes of formal
organization. For a while Frothingham seemed to be wavering and
Abbot feared that it would be necessary to issue a new call completely
independent of the Bartol conferences. But during this period of furious writing, speech making, and organizational disturbances in local
parishes and associations, Abbot put such fears aside. The committee
went forward with its plans for a program and obtained the consent
of a panel of prospective officers.

They scheduled the meeting for Anniversary Week, which was a
festive time in the Boston-Cambridge area with Harvard graduates
and Unitarians converging for various meetings both social and ecclesiastical. In due season the announcement was made in the press.

A PUBLIC MEETING

To Consider the Conditions, Wants, and Prospects of Free Religion
in America, will be held on Thursday, May 30, at 10 A.M. at Horticultural Hall, Boston. The following persons have been asked to address the meeting, and addresses may be expected from most of them:

Ralph Waldo Emerson
         John Weiss [a radical, Transcendentalist Unitarian]
      Robert Dale Owen [a "scientific" Spiritualist]

---

[22]Potter, *Historical Address*, 12.

> Wm. H. Furness [a moderate Unitarian]
> Lucretia Mott [a liberal Quaker]
> Henry Blanchard [a liberal Universalist]
> T. W. Higginson [a Transcendentalist, ex-Unitarian
> Free Religionist]
> D. A. Wasson [Transcendentalist, Free Religionist]
> Isaac M. Wise [liberal rabbi, Cincinnati]
> Oliver Johnson [a "Progressive Friend" (Quaker)]
> F. E. Abbot [a scientific theist, positivist]
> Max Lilienthal [liberal rabbi, Cincinnati]

Outwardly, the meeting was an immense success: Horticultural Hall was filled to overflowing by an enthusiastic throng, and the strategy of having Emerson speak last kept the audience in its place to the end. Critics taunted the sponsors with the observation that the most prominent feature of the meeting was the absence of unity, cohesion, or agreement. But the radicals could say that despite the diversity of the views presented, they had at least provided a platform for the free discussion of religious questions. In general, the response by both leaders and the public was sufficient to inspire hope and confidence that the enactments of the afternoon business meeting would offer promise of a rich and useful future for the Free Religious Association.[23]

The business meeting was conducted without acrimony or controversy; the proposed constitution was adopted without substantial changes; and a slate of officers was elected. When the meeting closed and enrollment of members began (Emerson's dollar being accepted first and his name put at the head of the list), the F.R.A. had been put in the hands of a diversified but capable group of men and women who, however much in disagreement on methods and conclusions, were united in their dissatisfaction with creeds and orthodoxies, and enthusiastic in their praise of freedom.

The F.R.A. was never large and its destiny was controlled during its first (and most active) decade by less than two dozen men and women. A résumé of the views and the backgrounds of the leaders, therefore, goes far to clarify the nature and function of the organization. The primary fact about the F.R.A. is that it was a revolt from and within Unitarianism. It did make an appeal beyond the denomination, to be sure, but all of the clergymen holding major offices dur-

---

[23]Persons, *Free Religion,* 45-49, contains a more detailed account of the meeting. Cf. also *Report of Addresses at a Meeting Held in Boston, May 30, 1867, to Consider the Conditions, Wants, and Prospects of Free Religion in America* (Boston, 1867); and Potter, *Historical Address,* 14-15.

ing the first decade (except Rabbi Wise) had been ordained Unitarians. At the same time nearly all of the lay men and women had been at one time, or remained, similarly affiliated. The ecumenical character of the first (1867) convention soon disappeared and the only significant shift came with the influx of materialists, atheists, and persons antagonistic to what could be called a religious view of life.

Emerson, who was a vice-president as long as he lived, was the patriarch of the Free Religionists and the "great emancipator" of American theology. Along with Theodore Parker, Emerson stood highest in the radical pantheon. Even though Parker was dead, his influence was probably more direct. Parker's activism and fervor, no less than his long-running battle with Unitarianism, made him a more compelling object of radical admiration. He had "converted" Frothingham back in the antislavery days, and almost all the others saw him as both hero and martyr of the radical cause.

The abolitionist tradition is another vital factor. Potter was not the only one who saw the F.R.A. as an intellectual counterpart to what was then regarded as the gloriously victorious crusade against chattel slavery. Nor can anyone adequately evaluate the power of the abolition mystique on the generation who had seen the great cause of black emancipation rise from the demand of a few outraged and hated enthusiasts to the battle cry of a nation in arms, and who were to see that cause culminate in three amendments to the Constitution. Again Parker was the hero, and Vice-Presidents Gerrit Smith, Lucretia Mott, and Lydia Maria Child had been leaders as well, while almost all of the others had taken lesser parts in the antislavery movement. As this last group suggests, the same factors that linked abolitionism with the agitation for women's rights brought a large feminine component into the F.R.A. leadership.

There were always a few Jews in the list of officers, but Rabbi Isaac M. Wise of Cincinnati was the most active in the first decade, even though there were several other Jews who took part in various public activities. Wise was a radical who went well beyond most of the reform rabbis in America in his demands for modern, rational religion. Robert Dale Owen, son of the New Harmony socialist and leading light of American Spiritualism, remained continually interested in the association, reflecting the general liberal tendencies of the then large and well-organized Spiritualist movement in the country. Finally there was a small group of interested laymen, businessmen for the most part, who revealed great loyalty to Free Religion but who never considered themselves more than amateurs in the field of religious thought.

In general, it can be said that most of the leaders and supporters of the association were marginal members of the liberal denominations (particularly the Unitarian) who were uneasy under doctrinal restrictions. Transcendentalism provided the chief intellectual inspiration though scientific philosophers such as Comte, Spencer, and Huxley gave a positivistic orientation to the thought of many. Nearly all were genuinely desirous of some formal religious affiliations and almost none was openly antireligious. To such persons, the F.R.A. facilitated a genteel departure from confessional religion.

Just what was the purpose of the Free Religious Association? That was a question insistently asked by both members and opponents through the two decades of its most active existence. In explicit terms few agreed, yet in a general way they had a common objective. The first article of the constitution made some things clear:

> I. This Association shall be called the Free Religious Association,— its objects being to promote the interests of pure religion, to encourage the scientific study of theology, and to increase fellowship in the spirit; and to this end, all persons interested in these objects are cordially invited to its membership.[24]

The founders were incessantly speaking of "fellowship in the spirit," though it is never clear just what they meant by the phrase. Perhaps the vagueness was considered desirable. Perhaps what they wanted most was the right—and the occasion—to discuss theology and philosophy without restriction, and to follow the inquiry wherever it led. In any event, the second article further clarified the ideal of freedom and indirectly constituted a reproach to the various religious denominations whence the members came.

> II. Membership in this Association shall leave each individual responsible for his own opinions alone, and affect in no degree his relations to other associations. Any person desiring to co-operate with the Association shall be considered as a member, with full right to speak in its meetings; but an annual contribution of one dollar shall be necessary to give a title to vote,—provided also, that those thus entitled, may at any time confer the privilege of voting upon the whole assembly, on questions not pertaining to the management of business.

---

[24]The constitution is printed in each issue of the F.R.A. *Proceedings*. In 1873, largely due to the objections of Lucretia Mott, this article was broadened to call for "a scientific study of man's religious nature and history," rather than simply theology. The implications of this change will be seen in the alienation of Abbot from the intuitionists, discussed in ch. 9.

Yet not even the most garrulous wanted an organization that provided *only* for the exchange of views. Potter probably stated the matter most accurately when he said in 1875 that the association "aims
to render [service] of that kind which works upon public opinion, in
the general direction of free and rational thought in religion, through
the influence of the written or spoken word." In that report (written
by Potter) the Executive Committee specifically eschewed active
work, or the solution of problems issuing from local or special exigen-
cies, or the "establishment of a network of local organizations for ef-
fecting this or that definite and tangible purpose."[25] It is this mission
of intellectual advocacy—not even widespread popular propagandiz-
ing—that must be described and evaluated in a consideration of the
association's contribution.

The F.R.A. during the first ten years of its existence never undertook an overly ambitious program. The first report of the Executive Committee reveals essentially the scope of the organization. It
had corresponded with certain fellow spirits in other countries, organized a series of ten lectures in Cambridge, published a report of the
1867 meeting, projected a program of tract and book publication, and
arranged an extensive program for the annual Boston convention.

For all practical purposes the scope and function of the association
was never substantially broadened. Despite certain efforts to deepen
or extend its nature and influence, it never became a primary allegiance of its members, and all of its officers had other duties. In this
respect, Abbot was no exception. As editor of the *Index* and president
of the National Liberal League, Abbot advanced the propositions an-
nunciated by the F.R.A. and exerted strenuous efforts to make it a
more militant organization, but his primary loyalties were elsewhere.
Potter, who was the association's most devoted servant, remained
minister of the New Bedford church and served as director of both the
Index Association and the National Liberal League. The chief agents
used to fulfill the association's function were the lecture, the public
convention, and the printing press, but as a number of individuals
noted, it had consistently been "a voice without a hand."[26] Moreover,
as the years went by its voice was less heard, and other organizations
took up its message. It is worthwhile nevertheless to consider briefly
the work that it *did* try to do. Only during its first decade, however,

---

[25]*F.R.A. Proceedings, 1875,* 7-8.

[26]Potter, *Historical Address,* 19.

was it a vital or influential organization; after its second decade it was moribund.

During its first ten years the association published eight tracts and two books. These publications included Samuel Johnson on the worship of Jesus, William H. Channing (nephew and biographer of the great Unitarian patriarch) on the religions of China, and a number of tracts on the taxation of church property, sabbatarianism, and the public school question. *Freedom and Fellowship in Religion: A Collection of Essays and Addresses* by various F.R.A. leaders was projected in 1868. It was brought together largely through the efforts of Potter, though he was aided by Abbot, who constantly advocated that the book become an antidote to "Free Religious Orthodoxy." To prevent the formation of a mere "radical sect," Abbot even thought that at least one essay should be "atheistic, but in good spirit."[27] As finally published seven years later, the volume contained contributions by Wasson, Samuel Longfellow (Transcendentalist and brother of the poet), Samuel Johnson, Weiss, Potter, Abbot, Frothingham, Ednah D. Cheney, and others. *Freedom and Fellowship* was by no means broad and universal in outlook. Abbot himself was the only outspoken positivist, while Ednah Dow Cheney—who had been involved in antislavery, freedmen's aid, and women's rights—was the only one who could be considered in any sense an active reformer. The volume as a whole was irenic and urbane—an expression of post-Emersonian liberalism. In addition to this publication, the *Proceedings* of the annual meetings, complete with addresses, were published for public sale. Especially in the early years, the meetings received extensive coverage in the religious periodicals and the newspapers of the time. Most of the lectures were published verbatim in the major Boston and New York dailies.

The lecture series and the public conventions were always the most effective instruments. The success of these methods was attested by the wide interest in the first meeting in May 1867, and reinforced by the alarm in Orthodox circles created by a series of lectures that Potter sponsored in Cambridge during the academic year 1867-1868. This series (to which Abbot contributed a paper) was repeated in part in Boston and led to the invitations to Weiss and Frothingham to become class preachers at the Divinity School in 1868 and 1869.[28] In later years lectures were presented in three different ways: the an-

---

[27]FEA to Potter, 18 March 1868.

[28]*F.R.A. Proceedings, 1868,* 8; Persons, *Free Religion,* 79.

nual Boston meetings, the Horticultural Hall lecture series, and Free
Religious conventions held in various Eastern and Northern cities. The
Boston meetings were the most important not only because of the attention they attracted but for their cohesive effect on the membership.

The most important part of the Annual Meeting, however, was the
convention; after 1870 the Boston meetings became less a platform
for all religious liberals than for the Free Religious movement as such.
This did not mean, of course, that disagreements in the F.R.A. itself
were not aired. Abbot, as long as he remained active in the organization, was involved in exacerbating the cleavages between intuitionalists and positivists.[29]

The sessions of 1873 illustrate the nature of the F.R.A.'s platform
after its scope had been narrowed. On this occasion Samuel Johnson
(the old Free Religionist, intuitionalist, and student of Oriental religion), William C. Gannett (the Unitarian anticreedalist and biographer of his father, Ezra Stiles Gannett), Robert Dale Owen, T. W.
Higginson, Samuel Longfellow, Lucretia Mott, and Abbot joined in a
concerted attack on evangelical, or even liberal, religion. Their points
of view were, of course, varied—and Owen did little but cite reviews
that approved his recent volume of apologetics for Spiritualism. At this
meeting there was no deference to the Christ, only occasional eulo-
gies of Jesus the man. The speakers were unanimously on radical
ground.

The "autumnal" conventions sponsored by the F.R.A. in cities
other than Boston followed generally the same pattern, though it can
be said that these conventions represented more clearly the Free Religionist point of view. The Executive Committee recommended incorporating this as a part of the association program in its report of
1870. In 1871, 1872, and 1873 two or three cities were reached. The
success of these meetings, usually held in rented halls and sometimes
against resistance from local churches, varied. The two-day meetings
in the West during November 1870 were enthusiastically attended,
as were the Syracuse meetings in 1871. The meetings in Detroit in
December 1871 were ill fated, however. The weather was so fiercely
cold that the hall could not be brought above forty-two degrees. "The
speakers, muffled in overcoats, with little clouds of breath issuing from
their mouths as they spoke, yet spoke on; the hearers sat, outwardly
frigid, but with occasional demonstrations of inward warmth, and few

---

[29]Report of the Executive Committee, *F.R.A. Proceedings, 1870*, 10-11.

went out."[30] One hundred fifty of those remaining finally retired to a warmer room. Certainly the most publicized convention was that held in Cooper Union, New York, immediately after the tumultuous ten-day convocations of the Evangelical Alliance, which had brought 20,000 people to its various meetings on the closing night. The most specific of all of the convention programs was that in Boston (1877), when the speakers all concentrated on the "Sunday question."

The Horticultural Hall Lecture Series was a special project sponsored by the F.R.A. for Boston. The idea was an old one, an extension of the lyceum courses that had been meeting the insatiable New England demand for public lecture-instruction for decades. Abbot and other F.R.A. speakers took part in Samuel Longfellow's Parker Fraternity series in 1868. A year later the Horticultural Hall lectures were begun, and continued in 1870, under the direction of Edwin Morton, a Boston attorney. It was not until 1871 that this lecture series was taken over by the F.R.A., and even then it was arranged and paid for with funds raised by R. P. Hallowell, who was a partner in a firm of Boston Wool Commission merchants.

The subject matter of the lectures reflected for the most part the ideological position of the association. Despite their being given in a period of unusual economic and social stress, the lectures were speculative and historical, Emersonian rather than Garrisonian in spirit. Only occasional contributions on the Sabbath problem, secularism, and the "woman question" varied a pattern that was theoretical rather than practical. Yet the quality of these lectures was good. Abbot was hardly exaggerating when he said that they brought to the platform "the ripest and most carefully matured thought of the ablest and most distinguished advocates of religious radicalism who are now before the American public."[31]

The discontinuation of the Horticultural Hall series after 1879 was merely one of many indications that the Free Religious Association closed the first and most important phase of its history between the years 1878 and 1880. By that time the series had lost all the savor that came with being revolutionary. Its more energetic members, such as Abbot or Wendell Phillips, in very different ways expressed their primary convictions through other channels. After 1880 as before, Potter remained the soul of the movement, and kept it in quiet paths until his death in 1893. Thomas Wentworth Higginson succeeded

---

[30] *F.R.A. Proceedings, 1871,* 10-11; *Index,* 30 December 1871.

[31] *Index,* 30 December 1871.

Potter and continued his program. After she resigned, Ednah Dow Cheney, who had been a loyal member and leader of the association from the beginning, could well reflect on the fact that by 1902 its job was done. "The best of all is that we hope we are becoming useless, for the spirit of free religion is fast permeating all the societies. How much of it is due to our special efforts we do not care to estimate, but we feel that, as an advance guard, we still have our place in importance."[32] Her words could almost as well have been written in 1880.

---

[32]Ednah Dow Cheney, *Reminiscences* (Boston: Lee and Shepard, 1902) 147-49.

CHAPTER SIX

TOLEDO AND THE INDEX

DURING THE SPRING OF 1868 while Abbot was giving private tuition to suspended Harvard students and journeying to Dover on weekends to preach, he was also giving consideration to various offers for resettlement. A clerical position was hard to find, however, and for a time he even gave consideration to selling insurance. The Reverend Daniel Bowen, another one of the "excluded," had done likewise, speaking of "the philanthropic character of the institution of Life Insurance" as one of the "great instrumentalities of our day for binding together in a practical way human society for mutual benefit."[1] Two years after this Frank turned to the same institution in desperation, but was dissuaded by his close friend from college days, Albert Stickney, now a successful New York attorney.

Not everyone lost interest in Abbot, even though he thought that his days as a settled minister were over. During the winter of 1868-1869 the Unitarian Society of Toledo, Ohio, became interested in him. The connecting link in this instance was an old classmate from Meadville, the Reverend Stephen H. Camp, who was minister there but was moving to the 3rd Society of Brooklyn. David Ross Locke—editor of the Toledo *Blade,* author of the famous "Petroleum V. Nasby Letters," and a member of the Toledo Society—paid a visit to Abbot during this winter and was impressed. Negotiations were begun the following May with a formal request for a trial period of preaching that painted an attractive picture.

> It is perhaps the freest organization in the West calling itself Unitarian, no creed, no communion service has obtained for years. We are a radical people and desire a progressive preacher, no disposition to dictate or limit his scope of thought will be found among us. Financially the church may be said to be in a flourishing condition. . . . A fine brick church is in the process of construction and will be finished next year.[2]

---

[1] Bowen to FEA, 13 March 1867.

[2] A. E. Macomber to FEA, 8 May 1869. See also Camp to FEA, 7 May 1869.

Abbot answered with his usual firmness. He indicated his desire to come, but gave some strict stipulations: that union with the National Conference be severed and that the name Unitarian (which had been the crucial thing at Dover) be abandoned.

Both Stephen Camp and A. E. Macomber (another of the leading members of the society) answered. The departing minister gave fair warning that it was not strong enough to stand division.[3] Macomber, on the other hand, reported that Abbot's *Examiner* article on "The Ethics of Pulpit Instruction" had been circularized and that the society had nevertheless voted unanimously to request him as a candidate preacher. Abbot accepted the invitation, stating that he could not begin his series of sermons until the first Sunday in July. (His private students required his presence up until the time of Harvard's entrance examinations.)

Late in June the Abbot family, with various members of the Abbot kin to see them off, left on the train from Boston. Frank went with Katie and the children as far as Chicago; from there they journeyed alone to the Mississippi and then up to Winona. Abbot then went back to Toledo alone, being enthusiastically greeted by the Toledo *Blade* as having "[few superiors] among the young men of our time in the department of metaphysics."[4] He took up rooms in a boardinghouse where he spent most of two sweltering months writing a series of sermons on the problems of Christianity and Free Religion. Frank also took time to become acquainted with the city and the intrepid society that had summoned him.

Toledo in 1869 was a mushrooming Western city whose amazing growth easily explains the enthusiasm of one of its boosters, who wrote *A Presentation of the Future Great City of the World in the Central Plain of North America: Showing That the Centre of the World's Commerce, Now Represented by the City of London, Is Moving Westward to the City of New York, and Thence, within One Hundred Years, to the Best Position on the Great Lakes.* Climate, soil, trade routes, and the destiny of America were to make this present rival of Chicago, located on the banks of the Maumee, "the true claimant for this high destiny."[5] For a time at least, statistics seemed to justify such enthusiasm. A town of 3,829 in 1850, Toledo had grown to 13,768 by

---

[3]Camp to FEA, 19 May 1869.

[4]Toledo *Blade*, 3 July 1869.

[5]J. W. Scott, 2d rev. ed., 1876, 32.

1860, and 31,584 by 1870. In 1880 Toledo's population would reach 50,137. In such a sprawling and transitional metropolis the prospect for Free Religion would seem to have been exceedingly bright.

The Unitarian Society had been organized in 1855, although Unitarian services had been held as early as 1838. Three ministers had served the congregation so far. Like most Unitarian congregations its members were drawn from families prominent in business, interested in civic advancement, and generally of New England or Eastern lineage. Abbot was later able to enlist the aid of many liberal, free-thinking Germans in the Index Association, but they were not prominent in the society at the time of his call. A. E. Macomber, looking back in 1923, remembered that Frank had been called by "a group of young men comprising a number of lawyers and solid business men."[6] A. D. Pelton was a publisher of the Toledo *Blade;* Edward Bissell, son of a millionaire railroad magnate and founder of the Erie and Kalamazoo railroads, was one of the city's most prominent attorneys and a commissioner in his father's railroad. Calvin Cone was a division superintendent of the United States Express Company; Fred A. Jones was a judge of Probate Court; and there were at least two other judges in the parish. But the two most important leaders of the society were Macomber and David Ross Locke.

Albert E. Macomber was born in Taunton, Massachusetts, in 1837. He had come west as a young man and attended the Michigan Agricultural College and later the University of Michigan law school. In Toledo Macomber practiced law, but was primarily a real estate agent of very considerable means. He was a financial mainstay of the society and was sincerely interested in the kind of religious liberalism that Abbot advocated.

David Ross Locke was born in Vestal, New York, in 1833. He had begun working as a printer and then as printer-publisher of various small Western papers. Locke became a nationally famous figure during the Civil War when as editor of the Findlay (Ohio) *Jeffersonian* his "Petroleum V. Nasby" letters were published to confound the "copper-heads." In 1865 he came to Toledo and took the editorial chair of the *Blade.* Later, as its owner, he built its weekly edition into a nationally known periodical, in large part through his successful satires. Locke, however, was not only a political satirist and humorist, but a man deeply concerned about religion and ethics. One writer did call

---

[6]A. E. Macomber, *The Unitarian Church in Toledo* (Toledo: privately printed, 1923) 2.

him a "devoted Christian" and refers to "several hymns . . . which have taken a high place in our modern hymnology." In point of fact, though, Locke was not deeply interested in Christianity.[7] When asked if he was a pillar of the church, he answered that he was "a pillar of the portico. . . . I'm an outside support." He did, nonetheless, become one of Abbot's most enthusiastic supporters, and between 1869 and 1873 he succored Free Religion with some $6,000. Abbot was once referred to as "one of the favorite parishioners of Rev. P. V. Nasby."[8] Locke also attempted on occasion to turn his satirical talents to the cause, but Abbot found his pieces lacking in intellectual content and quietly discouraged further efforts.

Abbot's initial impression of the society was quite favorable, since it contained so many alert, intelligent, responsible, and liberal leaders. He considered the parish "ripe for the movement." In fact there were only three "born Unitarians" in the congregation, so they were unusually inclined to follow his radical counsels. Moreover, they continued to attend his regular services in large numbers, despite his flouting every convention of Protestantism. He omitted prayers, he closed services without the benediction, he used John Stuart Mill in lieu of a Scripture text, and delivered a series of sermons that were the most unconditional he had ever delivered. Nevertheless, Abbot wrote, "the society [was] evidently willing to take the bold, manly stand and hoist the flag of free religion." "Things go on swimmingly." The parishioners were "delighted." Abbot had also attracted the favor of the large German population by attacking a Congregationalist minister who had publicly objected to German festivities on the Sabbath. Moreover, it seemed that the financial circumstances were auspicious for liberalism since "the clean radicals are financially the leading men. . . . The real strength of the radicals both in numbers and in money is as *five to one*."[9]

There were difficulties, however. Henry W. Bellows and other Unitarian leaders had indicated to delegates of the Toledo Society that

---

[7]*Portrait and Biographical Record of the City of Toledo* (Chicago, 1895) 132.

[8]The *Christian Register,* 31 August 1872; Jack C. Ransome, "David Ross Locke, The Post-War Years," *Northwest Ohio Quarterly* 20 (Summer 1948): 155. See also Cyril Clemens, *Petroleum Vesuvius Nasby* (Webster Groves MO: International Mark Twain Society, 1936).

[9]FEA to Katie, 19, 27 July 1869; FEA to Horsch, 12 July; 22 August 1869.

their invitation to Abbot prejudiced their standing as a Unitarian society. The *Liberal Christian,* the New York Unitarian magazine that Bellows controlled, openly criticized Abbot for "candidating" in a Christian church.[10] In a more direct manner the former minister, Stephen H. Camp, was influencing affairs by letting it be known that he thought a vote against Unitarianism jeopardized his relationship with his present parish in Brooklyn. Camp wielded his influence even more directly by appearing on the scene and actively though quietly working for the defeat of Abbot's demands. Nonetheless, the most important opposition came from the steadfast conservative members, who simply did not wish to have their society depart from the fold of Christendom. These people were enthusiastic about Abbot personally, for on 8 August—at a meeting "larger and more enthusiastic than the Society had ever had"—they decided by a vote of 60 to 2 to call him. Significantly, "by a mistake or over-conciliatory feeling," two of the conservatives succeeded in having this vote taken without having a vote on Abbot's resolutions to sever Unitarian connections.[11]

Under the circumstances Abbot considered acceptance utterly out of the question, and on the following Sunday (15 August) with his resolutions as his text he delivered a sermon, "Unitarianism vs. Freedom," which stated explicitly why this separation was necessary from his point of view. "That sermon satisfied and convinced every strong mind in the Society of the necessity of my position," wrote Abbot.[12] He announced that on the following Sunday this matter would have to be put to another vote, and a week of caucusing, tension, and contention followed. It became perfectly apparent soon enough that the previous vote (60 to 2) was in no way an indication of general sentiments on the larger question. "It is party spirit, and ill-temper aroused by Camp on his visit, that lies at the bottom of the fuss," Abbot remarked, but this was too simple an explanation. Those who had opposed the resolutions had always regarded themselves as members of a Christian Church; they considered it blasphemy to suggest that their old allegiance had been undeserved; and they resisted the trend toward Free Religion—or infidelity, as they no doubt thought—with the fervor of loyal Unitarians. It is not surprising that during the special subscription held on 9 August to assure a salary for Abbot, only $50

[10]FEA to Katie, 19 July 1869.

[11]Diary, 9 August 1869; FEA to Horsch, 25 August 1869.

[12]FEA to Horsch, 15 August 1869.

of the $2,250 raised came from those who would later demonstrate their Christian sympathies.[13]

On Sunday, 22 August, the test came; by a vote of 38 to 18 the resolutions were passed without amendment and a formal call was extended to Abbot. "We have fired the shot heard round the world," Frank wrote his wife. "The Unitarian conspiracy of silence is defeated and the New Reformation fairly begun."[14] Recognizing this as "the first popular verdict pronounced on the conflicting claims of Christianity and Free Religion," Abbot accepted the call. On the following Sunday, he inaugurated the "new epoch" with a sermon on "The Ministry of Free Religion."

The "New Reformation," however, ran into the usual difficulties immediately. One member resigned from the board, and another, the "chief of the conservative party," withdrew from the society altogether. Others either followed suit or threatened to, and soon there was "considerable talk of a new Unitarian Society." There were continuing rumors of distant encouragement for the conservatives from Camp, and later it became clear that they were receiving direction from Charles Lowe of the A.U.A.

Thus began Abbot's troubled ministry at Toledo. Although coming to the Toledo Society in search of rest and quiet, Abbot's uncompromising radicalism produced the same result there as it had in Dover. A new society was established, the "First Unitarian Society," which sapped severely the strength of Abbot's small society. This is not to say that his own endeavors in any way diminished. Indeed, a catalogue of his activities during these years shows the range of Abbot's interests. He delivered an oration to celebrate the German victory over the Second Empire of France, though later his conscience forced a recantation, whereupon he decried Imperial Germany's opposition to the French republicans in a second lecture. Abbot led local campaigns against using the Bible in the schools and for a program of evening education. He was bitterly denounced for delivering a Free Religious homily to the inmates of the Detroit House of Correction. Yet despite (or even perhaps because of) these public activities Abbot's parish duties gradually diminished and finally disappeared, and the vicissitudes of what were now the two branches of the old society did much to condition his career in the city. The fate of neither or-

---

[13]Diary, 23 September; 30 August 1869.

[14]FEA to Katie, 23 August 1869.

ganization was happy. Indeed, regarding Abbot's society this was almost inevitable, and long before he left in 1873 the society was failing.

Abbot's personal attitude toward the role of the ministry does much to explain the progressive decline of the society. Even had he not had other interests, he would have done little to foster organizational growth. Moreover, the opportunity to hear a philosopher deliver highly intellectualized weekly lectures on a vast variety of subjects from "The Compensations of Grief" to the "Hebrew Prophets" to "Capital Punishment" (a typical series of three delivered in the winter of 1869-1870) provided insufficient stimulation to parish esprit. Abbot's sermons, when he was not defending his own actions with a detailed historical résumé, were philosophical essays. Only on a few occasions did he depart from his regular practice of reading them. From the point of view of subject matter, his sermons rarely departed from a polemic spirit. Abbot inspired people by his integrity and by his intellectual force, but he was neither inclined nor capable of using the devices of eloquence, rhetoric, or poetry as did O. B. Frothingham for his huge congregation in New York. Fiscal problems soon developed and within a year, regular Sunday meetings had been discontinued.

The "free church" of Toledo was to go the same way as other Free churches in Worcester, Lynn, Barre, Watertown, Groveland (Massachusetts), and Rowland Connor's Society in Boston, not to mention the now-shrunken "Music Hall" Society Theodore Parker had founded. Most of these societies had arisen or prospered around a single colorful or dynamic man such as T. W. Higginson, Samuel Johnson, or O. B. Frothingham. They fell into various stages of desuetude when that leader left or died. In Abbot's case, even the commanding personality was lacking. Abbot himself readily recognized that he was neither intellectually nor emotionally adapted for "society building." The fundamental misconception was one that Potter well realized: Free thought could not be institutionalized according to a pattern established by two millennia of Christian "confessionalism." It was an ill-fated attempt to pour new wine into old bottles.[15] By 1873 the Toledo Society was largely moribund and Abbot and his family had moved back east to Boston.

Yet Abbot's Toledo years did have one major consequence. A national periodical of Free Religion was begun. A journalistic project had

---

[15]*Index*, 24 September 1870. See too, Persons, *Free Religion*, 26ff., and Ralph V. Harlow, *Gerrit Smith* (New York: H. Holt and Co., 1939) 193ff.

long been under consideration. Early in July of 1869 the idea of a magazine of some sort had been suggested by some people among Abbot's congregation. This idea had clearly met with Abbot's approval, and during his trip east he received support from other leaders, notably O. B. Frothingham and William J. Potter. By 1 November the prospectus for this new periodical, the *Index,* was written. Since the *Index* provides such an important insight into the perimeter of Free Religious sensibilities at the time, an examination of its editorial position constitutes the rest of this chapter.

The fundamental thrust of the *Index* was clearly delineated in the prospectus that was distributed before its publication and printed in the first issue.

> The *Index* will aim at a two-fold object, positive and negative. It will aim, above all things, to increase pure and genuine *religion* in the world,—to develop a nobler spirit and higher purpose both in society and the individual. It will aim, at the same time, to increase *freedom* in the world,—to destroy every species of spiritual slavery, to expose every form of superstition, to encourage independence of thought and action in all matters that concern belief, character or conduct. It will, in short, be devoted to the cause of *free religion,* which it proposes to advocate with the utmost ability and moral earnestness it can command. . . . Its only policy will be strong thought and plain speech. It will neither seek nor shun to "shock" the religious nerve. Standing squarely outside of Christianity, it will yet aim to be just to it, recognizing its excellencies, noting its defects. It will pay no deference to the authority of the Bible, the Church, or the Christ, but rest solely on the authority of right reason and good conscience. It will trust no revelation but that of universal human faculties. It will accept every certified result of science, philosophy, and historical criticism, asking no question what it proves. Briefly, it will seek the truth and work for humanity.[16]

The *Index* never turned from these aims, even though it proved in some respects impossible to keep it on the high intellectual level that the prospectus suggested. "Plain speech" and "strong thought" were seldom lacking; but due to the ever-present menace of bankruptcy and the fever pitch of many conflicts, there were times—unfortunately many times—when the aim "to develop a nobler spirit" or "to create intellectual and spiritual unity" was shunted into the

[16]*Index,* 1 January 1870.

background. Yet given its conditions of publication, these shortcomings were virtually inevitable.

Periodicals of the day frequently observed that "Abbot *was* the *Index*." From the beginning to the end this was, indeed, explicitly the case. The paper was never an avocation for Abbot. In part this was because his temperament and outlook made any delegation of responsibility impossible. "I distrusted organizations," he wrote, and as a consequence all manner of detail fell on his shoulders. Not only did Abbot write most of the copy, he performed all of the proofreading and he made decisions concerning the most detailed business and technical matters. Moreover, he always gave personal attention to correspondence received; and when out of town, he insisted that Mrs. Abbot open the daily mail and keep him informed of developments. Nor did Abbot ever diminish the thoroughness with which he studied the American Protestant, Catholic, and liberal religious press. Abbot devoted almost one day a week to this (to him) loathsome task, and the pages of the *Index* attest to the closeness of his examination. Before long he was being "worked half to death." Yet he faced the circumstances with a spirit of determination and a confidence in his endurance that proved to be too optimistic.[17]

A fundamental problem was the continuing shortage of new or original writing. This resulted both from the enormous demands for articles that a weekly publication created and the lack of a sufficiently large contributors' fund. Abbot's contribution soon was reduced to editorials, sermons, and lectures that were almost always written for delivery elsewhere and were frequently narrow in application. The *Index* was similarly unable to attract much more·than sermons and occasional lectures from other Free Religious leaders. The main exceptions to this rule were the F.R.A. convention addresses, the Horticultural Hall lectures, and various Liberal League addresses, which found through the *Index* a larger audience very similar to that which heard the spoken words.

Lacking original articles, the *Index* was increasingly driven to reprint various types of secondhand matter. Many essays were taken from the British *Fortnightly Review* or *Westminster Review*. Others were the published works of a wide array of authors who could in one way or another be classified as anti-Christian or secular-minded. John Stuart Mill, David Hume, Max Müller, John Tyndall, T. H. Huxley, or David Friedrich Strauss were typical of the better type of writers.

---

[17]FEA to Horsch, 21 January 1870.

But along with these great works were frequent selections from Wiley Britton, who wrote on various scientific and philosophic problems, and a very extensive serialization of the eccentric Stephen Pearl Andrews's *Basic Outline of Universology.*

Abbot, of course, was aware of these faults as well as of their cause. Though it took him a decade to discover that this was not his vocation, he lamented from the first that he had to face "the transient toils—the tiresome task of teaching the world ideas that to me are ABC."[18] As for Abbot's own development, the unfortunate fact remains that he did not refine his thinking during these years. Events crystallized some views and forced certain conclusions, but except for a limited number of lectures (most of them for the annual Horticultural Hall series), Abbot's contributions to the *Index* do not reveal any significant advances in his philosophical conceptions.

The vexed relations between the *Index* and the Free Religious Association, which were not really resolved until the F.R.A. took over the *Index* in 1880, were also constricting in their effect. There is no doubt that the paper was at first conceived to be an unofficial organ of the F.R.A. since the promise of F.R.A. support had much to do with its establishment. During the first year, in fact, William J. Potter edited a weekly page devoted to association affairs; but this created so many misunderstandings about the independence of the paper that after the first year, F.R.A. notices were merely published as news and various leaders were enlisted as "editorial contributors." Even so the organizational lines remained indistinct and understood only by the more legalistic insiders. Considering the interlocking directorates and duplication of personnel, this is not surprising. Yet it did have the unfortunate result of demanding dozens of articles clarifying the distinctions, and affirming over and over again that neither Abbot or another "contributor" was representing anybody but himself. Had these disputes been prosecuted in private, there would have been less acrimony and dissension among the paper's constituency.

Yet one must not underestimate the importance of the paper. "The *Index* is an agitator," Abbot proclaimed, "its work is agitation, the strenuous endeavor to apply the highest religious ideas of the time to a state of society not yet brought up to their level."[19] These words characterize the dominant temper of the paper. On average its readers were thoughtful, though it was not a paper for intellectuals as had

---

[18]FEA to Katie, 18 July 1870.

[19]*Index*, 4 September 1873.

been the old *Christian Examiner* (1824-1869) or the shorter-lived *Radical* (1865-1872). The *Index* was dominated by a polemic spirit, trying to accomplish its ends not so much by philosophical and "scientific" criticism as by ridicule and castigation. Even though all voices interested in "true liberalism" were given a hearing in the pages, there was always sharp editorial criticism of articles that ran counter to Abbot's thinking. It became increasingly clear that there *was* a definite and affirmative *Index* position, but it was so pugnaciously and aggressively argued that it is most revealing to review its program in terms of what it was *against*. To this end a schema of the "circle" of the *Index*'s positions may be enlightening.

Christianity was the first object of *Index* attack because it represented the principle of Authority against Freedom, or in its less extreme manifestations, of Sentimentality against Reason. Although the sixteenth-century Reformation was seen as a great forward step, both Catholicism and orthodox Protestantism were pictured as menacing.

> Two vast powers have been growing up in the country during the hundred years just elapsed. One is the Catholic Power, in 1776 a mustard seed, in 1876 a tree overspreading the land. The other is the Evangelical Power, in 1776 a host of small and jealous sects, in 1876 a few rapidly consolidating denominations of immense wealth, numbers and influence.[20]

"Romanism," Abbot insisted, was the "natural development of Christianity," and throughout the controversy he waged in many issues of the *Index* with Francis W. Newman—a brother of the cardinal—who argued that it was a "corruption of Christianity," Abbot insisted that the Catholics were the most consistent Christians, and the Jesuits the most consistent Catholics.[21] Abbot therefore did not blame the Catholics for objecting to the Protestant monopoly of army or prison chaplaincies; he rather welcomed the embarrassment to officialdom that the Catholic demands created. But this in no way led him to consider them beneficent. "The Catholic Peril" was one of his most widely read editorials and one of the most frequently reprinted of the *Index* tracts. Catholic power was to be opposed both because of its own errors as well as for the reaction it would produce.

---

[20]"The Powers behind the Thrones," *Index,* 14 September 1876.

[21]Cf. "Romanism: The Natural Development of Christianity," *Index,* 11 May 1872 and Newman's article, "Romanism: A Corruption of Christianity," *Index,* 4 May 1872.

This, then, is the Catholic peril in America, not alone that the Roman
Catholic Church may become a ruling majority, or (what is worse) a
ruling minority, with all the measureless miseries and mischiefs of that
rule, but that, in order to strengthen the Republic against the possibility of such rulership, the great Protestant party may resort to measures involving a revolutionary subversion of the fundamental
principle of the Republic itself.[22]

This was the nature of Abbot's fear, and he was utterly uninterested in joining any of the "liberal" campaigns to support "American-
ist" movements within the Catholic Church itself. He thus wrote an
editorial on "The Catholic Conspiracy" in response to an article in the
same issue by the Reverend Samuel P. Putnam. Putnam urged liberals to support a Pennsylvania priest (Father Stack) in his fight for
trial before his peers in a controversy with Bishop O'Hara. Abbot was
unconcerned as to whether the Catholic Church would extend jurisdiction of the canon law to the United States. His solution was simple:
the principle of "absolutely secular government."[23]

In regard to the great evangelical host, Abbot's solution was the same
but his attack more satirical. The same secularist goals inspired the attack on chaplains, tax-exemption, or the Bible in the schools, but the
methods varied. A frequent argumentative device of Abbot consisted in
showing that Protestantism had not in fact abandoned what it professed
to abhor most in Romanism: authority and superstition. Less intellectual
was "The Sanctuary of Superstition," a weekly department consisting of
short evidences of Christian "primitivism" sent in by readers. Similar
were recurrent articles on prayer and miracles, many of them not much
more relevant than John Tyndall's widely advertised suggestion that the
efficacy of prayer be put to empirical test!

On many occasions such encounters were the cause of long campaigns of argument that served to drive from Abbot's following all the
more moderate liberals. These arguments now do much to reveal the
extremity of Abbot's departure from the Christian fold. The controversy with Washington Gladden in the *Independent* was typical of
many others. Taken together they explain how the conservative religious press of the day came to regard the *Index* as a diabolical force
in America. In this instance the issue was fundamental enough, but
the debate reveals Abbot's disappointing propensity for becoming in-

---

[22]"The Catholic Peril in America," *Index*, 15 September 1876.
[23]Ibid.

volved in issues that were, to say the very least, not germane to the Free Religious cause.

The conflict arose over a chance remark that Abbot made in an editorial criticizing the *Morning Star* (a Free Will Baptist journal published in Dover, New Hampshire) for praising a man who had demonstrated "the principle of making the cause of Christ first" by putting a foreign missions pledge above a bill for wood.[24] Abbot held that to make debts to God of higher obligation than debts to man is to enunciate a "pernicious" principle, but he complicated his argument with the gratuitous remark that it cost three dollars to send one dollar to the heathen. It was on this assertion that the *Independent* picked Abbot's article up, showing quite conclusively that this was not a true picture of overhead expenses in foreign missions. Abbot answered this charge by sidestepping his original claim and saying that he had merely used a popular adage; however, he still thought missionary work a very unremunerative effort.

> The whole system of foreign missions, judged by actual results, is a stupendous fraud upon credulous Christendom; and we speak only our most deliberate conviction when we say that the world would be incalculably better off without it. . . . In a word, humanity has today no worse enemy than the propagandist spirit of Christianity and the various ecclesiastical organizations it creates.[25]

Evangelical Protestantism, then, aroused deep apprehensions and provoked sharp, violent attacks that included even those great apostles of liberalism such as Henry Ward Beecher. These liberals, and particularly Unitarianism, occupy a special place in this connection.

Abbot was too involved in the Unitarian tradition to regard it as merely another department of Protestantism. From baptism to ordination Abbot had been nurtured in the Liberal Faith, taught to venerate its leaders, and encouraged to participate in the intellectual freedom it advocated. When Abbot chose to follow "the strong bent of his spirit," these same Liberal Faith followers ungraciously turned upon him, evicted him from his church, and continued both in pulpit and in press to heap ridicule and censure on his Free Religious efforts. Because many of the most loyal editorial contributions were recruited from men who had suffered a similar fate at authoritarian hands, and because the F.R.A. in a general way and Abbot's two In-

---

[24]*Index,* 13 May 1871.

[25]Ibid., 2 September 1871.

dependent Societies in a specific way had encroached on Unitarian ground, events frequently revealed mutually vindictive attitudes.

The *Index* sustained a continuous critical exposure of Unitarian activities that seemed to reveal the incompatibility of their joint ideal of freedom and faith. The leitmotiv of its analysis was the running commentary provided on that memorable pronouncement of Frederic Hedge: "I do maintain that Christian churches, as organized bodies of believers, must stand or fall with the Christian Confession,— that is, the Confession of Christ as divinely human Master and Head."[26] With all the vehemence that his deep personal involvements and disappointments stimulated, Abbot entered this area of controversy. He republished almost all of his most controversial sermons, and many of them such as his *Farewell Sermons* at Dover more than once. He carried the matter into the Boston Radical Clubs, the Cambridge "Theological" Club, and innumerable informal discussions. The issue became one of the central passions of his life: "If you want freedom, you must abandon Christianity."

Nor was Abbot any more tolerant of a mediating group of Unitarians, the "Neo-Christians"; for them he parceled out a different kind of criticism. "Neo-Christian" was the name given to people who repudiated in toto the Messianic or evangelical nature of Christianity; who classed the Bible (along with the Koran and the Bhagavad-Gita) as fine wisdom literature; and who considered Jesus, Socrates, and Buddha great ethical thinkers. This same group insisted, nevertheless, that historically the Christian contribution was profounder and more satisfying. By euphemism they also were able to retain most, if not all, of the traditional religious vocabulary: salvation (through character), the Kingdom of God (through the inspiration of Jesus' example), and so on. These were the "allegorical interpretations of Neo-Christianity" that Abbot ridiculed as sentimental, cowardly, and merely political. Typical of this group was the Reverend S. R. Calthrop of Syracuse who, though not "ruling out" other historical religions, found his own "special history" involved in Christianity and preferred it.[27] Lines cannot be accurately drawn, but certainly other venerable theists belong in this same general category of people who also had abandoned traditional Christianity but still preferred the wisdom of the Bible to any other. These individuals, virtually all of

---

[26]Frederic H. Hedge, *Reason in Religion* (Boston, 1865) 218.

[27]See Calthrop's Horticultural Address of 1874, reprinted in *Index*, 10 September 1874.

whom were Transcendental epigoni, objected strenuously to Abbot's
insistence on defining religion as "man's effort to improve himself,"
or his comparison of Jesus and Socrates with the result being, if anything, in favor of the Greek.[28]

As one swings around the arc of *Index* opponents, the next logical
category includes the Intuitionalists, the "graduates of Transcendentalism" who, according to O. B. Frothingham's estimate, comprised the
bulk of the F.R.A. membership.[29] The list of persons of this persua-
sion would be long and impressive, though it would also reveal innumerable doctrinal variations existing under the general rubric.
Abbot's war with the Free Religious wing of this "school" continued
throughout the decade. The two keynotes in this running battle were
sounded by Abbot from the rostrum of Horticultural Hall in February
1871 with his "Intuitionalism *versus* Science; or the Civil War in Free
Religion" and in March 1877 with "The Scientific Method in Religion"—the conclusion of a series of lectures on Edwards, Channing,
and Parker.

In this regard Abbot did not even spare the sensibilities of one of
the important parts of the Free Religious constituency, the Spiritualists. Spiritualism, stemming from the 1848 Fox family rappings in
Hydesville, New York, was by 1890 an organized denomination with
nearly 50,000 members, more than a half-million dollars in corporate
property, and 334 separate organizations. Yet by the 1870s Spiritualism was divided into two wings. The conservatives believed implicitly in communications with the other world and erected a basically
Christian and professedly biblical theology that reinterpreted the
miracles, messages, and resurrection of Jesus. The liberals were more
philosophically inclined and believed that extrasensory communication
was something that merited "psychical research." With the conservatives Abbot had predictably little patience, but with the liberals he
expressed some open sympathy, since where they were in the as-
cendence this group provided much aid to his secularist campaigns.
Despite some sympathy with their social views, Abbot nonetheless insisted upon examining the central Spiritualist tenets on the strictest
grounds of scientific verifiability.

This hostility to Intuitionalism did not, by any means, lead Abbot
to deny the contribution of Emerson. Emerson, who had been friendly

---

[28]Cf. F. E. Abbot, *Jesus and Socrates in the History of Religion* (Toledo,
1870). This was first delivered as a Horticultural Hall Address.

[29]Frothingham in an editorial, *Index,* 10 August 1872.

to Abbot ever since the latter's school-teaching days in Concord, had written several recommendations in various connections and made generous gifts on several occasions. When Emerson spoke at Harvard Divinity School in his old age, Abbot took his two sons so that they could have a living memory of the "great old warrior." In the *Index* he wrote a glowing encomium: "Ralph Waldo Emerson is the greatest legacy that God has yet bestowed on America, and . . . this will become more and more patent as our generations pass."[30] Nor was Abbot's devotion to Theodore Parker any less fervent. "He was as spotlessly pure in respect of courage, sincerity, and devotion to truth, as any man that ever breathed."[31] Abbot looked at the matter dialectically, however, and saw these men as having performed services of immense value in liberating religious thought from dogma. It was their successors, the men who made dogmatics out of Transcendentalism, who failed (in Abbot's terms) to see that science was the true vehicle for exploiting the freedom that Emerson valued.

Another aspect of Intuitionalism that Abbot resisted in later years was its extreme individualism. Individualism found sanction in conscience and gave none to reason or society, or in Abbot's favorite term, to the "Consensus of the Competent." He especially came to fear and hate (as we shall see) the "free love element" that seemed to be pushing liberalism into libertinism in the name of individual freedom. This was Abbot's battle with the "Antinomians," and in large part the spirit of his reasoning dates back to John Winthrop's struggle with Anne Hutchinson or Luther's with Johannes Agricola. Abbot was averting chaos, but in so doing he had to contend with the bitter opposition of longtime associates and contributors such as Elizur Wright, William H. Spencer, William D. LeSueur, Sidney H. Morse, and others. In the process a set of ideas and a catchphrase uttered first in an informal address to the Debating Society of the Harvard Divinity School became the keystone of the "Seven Ethical Laws of Rationalism" that took their place as "standing matter" in the *Index*.[32]

From this ground it is simple to understand objection in the *Index* to the "crude, raw infidelism" of Robert Ingersoll, whom Abbot referred to as the Dwight L. Moody of liberalism. No more appealing to an or-

---

[30]*Index*, 8 August 1878.

[31]Ibid., 8 January 1870.

[32]The idea of the "Consensus of the Competent" was elaborated in Abbot's address to the Harvard Divinity School reported in the *Index*, 6 March 1879; "Seven Laws," *Index*, 29 May 1879.

derly mind like Abbot's was the rampant "free thinking" that was expounded in the Boston *Investigator*. This weekly paper was "devoted to the development and promotion of universal mental liberty," edited by a belligerent freethinker named Horace Seaver, and published by Josiah P. Mendum, both of whom later allied with D. M. Bennett's *Truth Seeker* (in opposition to the *Index*) over the question of the Comstock laws. There were intimations of the rupture long before 1878, however.

The platform of the *Investigator* is well summed up in its dictum that "Free Religion is not as good as No Religion" and its confidence that "the march of mind is onward, and that Christianity and Free Religion, too, have got to come to an end. Neither of them is a finality."[33] This critique of Free Religion involved a fundamental misunderstanding of the "openness" of Abbot's positivism. Finally when Seaver attacked both the (Christian) *Independent* and the Free Religious *Index* on more or less the same grounds, Abbot's ire was aroused. Seaver's attack began a controversy that indicates what petty issues could sometimes preoccupy the *Index*. Abbot attacked, among other things, Seaver's glorification of "Infidelity," declaring that "no lover of truth is an infidel."

> Infidelity is faithlessness to that which ought to be obeyed—and to that alone. . . . The word they ought to prize, for the sake of the thing it stands for, is not "Infidelity" but *Fidelity*. Freethinker, Radical, Liberal, Rationalist, non-Christian, what you please; but "Infidel"—never![34]

The final major faction of American religiophilosophical thought that Abbot assaulted on all possible occasions was the Positivism that stemmed from Auguste Comte, Herbert Spencer, T. H. Huxley, John Tyndall, and innumerable lesser lights of this evolutionary school. That Abbot was in some sense a member of their party he made clear enough in a review of the Kant-oriented *Metaphysics* of Henry Longueville Mansel:

> The revolution started by Kant has nearly run its course. . . . The necessity of a new revolution is uneasily and vaguely felt by the great masters of modern science, although no thinker has yet arisen of sufficient speculative genius to satisfy the want. Herbert Spencer is only a John the Baptist.[35]

---

[33]*Investigator*, 28 March; 8 February 1871.

[34]*Index*, 1 April 1871; *Investigator*, 12 April 1871.

[35]*Index*, 12 August 1871.

But long before his *Index* years, Abbot had defined the nature of his dissent using the Spencerian synthesis.

Abbot's critique followed two main lines. He first urged that Spencer's materialistic reductionism was a gratuitous assertion unwarranted by the scientific evidence at hand, and that "the armies of science must march by parallel roads until such an [ontological connection between mind and matter] *is* proved. . . . We decline, therefore, to accept his philosophy as a true unification of the sciences, or a faithful exposition of genuine Positivism."[36] In Abbot's second article this object came closer to the form it later took in the thought of William James, for Abbot emphasized that Spencer's concepts of "internal organizing forces" were essentially not consistent with a purely mechanistic ontology. Since these forces were especially important in man, moreover, any adequate metaphysical system must deal with them more creatively than Spencer had.[37]

Abbot's second line of criticism stemmed from the first and was more specifically religious. He challenged the unphilosophical dogmatism in the Spencerian doctrine of the "Unknowable," emphasizing the inadequacy of predicating from this "Unknowable Force" only unity, omnipresence, and causation. To Abbot any adequate religious philosophy (or theology) must be theistic and must also predicate the infinity, eternity, self-existence, and personality of deity. He saw his justification in the perception "that mind is the noblest outcome of Nature. [Humanity] sees in Nature itself the expression of that which is not less, but more, than mind,—the self-utterance of that which is not below him, but eternally and infinitely above; and in this supreme conviction he finds the open secret of the universe."[38]

The *Index* attack thus had swung the full theological and philosophical arc from Roman Catholicism to materialism and agnostic positivism. Because the stand of the journal itself was often obscured by dissents on separate issues by various of the editorial contributors, there was no positive *Index* stand in all of these controversies nor, as later analysis will reveal, was there a broad Free Religious "party" or "school" with Abbot at its head. The main outlines of Abbot's per-

---

[36] Abbot, "Spencer's *First Principles*," *Christian Examiner* 80 (March 1866): 251-52.

[37] Abbot, "Spencer's *Principles of Biology*," *North American Review* 221 (November 1868): 403, 406, 420.

[38] Abbot, "Spencer's *First Principles*," 243, 254.

sonal views, however, were pronounced in clear and certain terms. Anti-Christianity and secularism were the major themes, and his own metaphysical position justified his attitude at every point. He called himself a "positivist in theology" and a "scientific theist," but neither of these identifications adequately expresses his confident rationalism, his profound conviction that an irrefutable ontological position could be defended, and that there could be a "science of Being" around which a complete philosophical structure might be erected. The Abbot of the *Index*—as dogmatic as any pope, the *Christian Register* asserted—was a neo-rationalist.

CHAPTER SEVEN

SECULARISM AND THE LIBERAL LEAGUE

NOT THE *INDEX*, however, but the now-little-remembered Liberal League movement was the objectification of the central idea in Abbot's thinking; it became as well the central experience of his public career. The "idea" had grown gradually, crystallizing only with his expulsion from the Dover Unitarian Society. This "idea" became basic to the *Index* platform and soon came to dominate the paper's pages. When the *Index* became the official organ of the National Liberal League in 1875, much (if not most) of the paper's financial support was diverted. As a result, internecine wars of the N.L.L. wrecked the paper entirely, broke Abbot's spirit, and ended his active participation in American liberal "movements."

Abbot's anti-Christian secularism, however, was not an immediate corollary of his departure from Christianity. As late as 1871 he insisted that the members of the Index Association "are simply not Secularists, nor in any sense representatives of Secularism."[1] But gradually, as Abbot studied the American religious press and ecclesiastical machinations, he worked out the implications of his initial premises. Despite his earlier "Neo-Christian" view that democracy was nothing but the Christian idea applied to politics, the most casual reader of almost everything he wrote after 1868 could not fail to observe that his analysis of the "genius of Christianity" forced him to regard the Christian Church, in any form, as a menace to freedom. From the beginning, therefore, there was much antiecclesiastical acrimony in the *Index*'s pages. The main emphasis during the first year, nonetheless, was intellectual, and the greatest public ferment was caused by Abbot's publication of W. H. Herndon's letter on Lincoln's religious skepticism and his own Horticultural Hall address on "A Comparison of Jesus and Socrates."[2] Abbot also made various attacks on "Romanism," but these attacks were such standard fare to the readers of the American religious press that little comment was

---

[1]*Index*, 7 January 1871.

[2]2 April 1870, of which 5,000 were printed and distributed.

aroused. The second year likewise featured frequent and violent controversies and a persistent, embittered attack on the faith and foibles of Protestantism.

Beginning in 1872 the *Index* embarked upon its program in earnest. The first issue of the year began with a full blast, announcing a vast petition to demand the secularization of America and setting forth an "Impeachment of Christianity." All possible grounds for misunderstanding the absolute nature of Abbot's antagonism were removed. "In the name of Human Intelligence, . . . In the name of Human Virtue, . . . In the Name of the Human Heart, . . . In the name of Human Freedom, and in the name of Humanitarian Religion" Abbot condemned Christianity

> because it stands stubbornly in the path of all human progress, blocking the way of every movement which aims at the enlargement of human life,—opposes, and has always opposed, every genuine reform in human affairs,—consults only the interests of its own creed, and sets its face like a flint against the purely secular education in which, by a quick instinct, it recognizes the most dangerous enemy of this creed.[3]

Abbot's militant secularism was further stimulated by "The National Association to Secure the Religious Amendment of the Constitution of the United States," which held its first organized annual convention that year (31 January-1 February 1872). It had been organized under evangelical auspices with the goal of amending the Constitution in some way so as to incorporate a Christian (or at least a religious) commitment. Abbot was one of many who attended the meetings and heard the ambitious plans for expansion. Those plans included public meetings, the organization of local societies, a petition to the U.S. Congress, and the founding of a weekly organ, *The Christian Statesman*, with T. P. Stevenson as editor. On returning to Toledo, Abbot was steeled in purpose and determined to invigorate his counter-offensive.

The *Index* for 4 February renewed the attack, and along with the New York *Jewish Times*, the Boston *Banner of Light* and *Investigator*, the Chicago *Present Age*, the Baltimore *Crucible*, and many other liberal periodicals supported the great secularist petition that was to be submitted by Senator Charles Sumner of Massachusetts.[4] Al-

---

[3]*Index*, 6 January 1872.

[4]Of the papers listed, all but the *Times* and the *Investigator* were Spiritualist papers. Regarding the petition, see Sumner to FEA, 1 February 1872.

though Abbot's hope for a million signatures was by no means reached, the *Investigator* reported in April that it had sent in more than 23,000 signatures and that the *Index* and *Banner of Light* had done even better, despite the fact that the major portion of American liberal Christianity did not seem to have rallied to Abbot's support.

January 1873 saw the appearance of a new *Index,* doubled in size and with a distinguished group of editorial contributors. The more conservative papers noticed something else that was new: a distinct change of tone in its editorial matter. "ORGANIZE! LIBERALS OF AMERICA!" sounded the *Index:* "The hour for action has arrived. The cause of freedom calls upon us to combine our strength, our zeal, our efforts."[5] Thereafter came a summons for the founding of local, secularist Liberal Leagues and the "Nine Demands of Liberalism," which defined the goals of organization and which for a decade constituted the central battle cry of the secularists. Since these demands have become so famous (or infamous), they deserve to be cited in full.

THE NINE DEMANDS OF LIBERALISM

1 We demand that churches and other ecclesiastical property shall no longer be exempted from taxation.
2 We demand that the employment of chaplains in Congress, in State Legislatures, in the navy and militia, and in prisons, asylums, and all other institutions supported by public money, shall be discontinued.
3 We demand that all public appropriations for sectarian educational and charitable institutions shall cease.
4 We demand that all religious services now sustained by the government shall be abolished; and especially that the use of the Bible in the public schools, whether ostensibly as a textbook or avowedly as a book of religious worship, shall be prohibited.
5 We demand that the appointment, by the President of the United States or by the Governors of the various States, of all religious festivals and fasts shall wholly cease.
6 We demand that the judicial oath in the courts and in all other departments of the government shall be abolished, and that simple affirmation under the pains and penalties of perjury shall be established in its stead.
7 We demand that all laws directly or indirectly enforcing the observance of Sunday as the Sabbath shall be repealed.

---

[5]*Commonwealth,* 18 November 1873; *Index,* 4 January 1873.

8 We demand that all laws looking to the enforcement of "Christian" morality shall be abrogated, and that all laws shall be conformed to the requirements of natural morality, equal rights, and impartial liberty.

9 We demand that not only in the Constitutions of the United States and of the several States, but also in the practical administration of the same, no privilege or advantage shall be conceded to Christianity or any other special religion; that our entire political system shall be founded and administered on a purely secular basis; and that whatever changes shall prove necessary to this end shall be consistently, unflinchingly, and promptly made.

They were praised or attacked—but always published—by virtually every religious paper in the country.

Nor, having declared war, did Abbot relinquish the offensive; every succeeding issue continued the barrage. The Christian amendment movement, tax exemption of churches, Bibles in the schools, chaplains in the army, missionary privileges on the Indian reservations—all became the objects of bitter castigation.

During the summer months of 1873, both Abbot and the *Index* relocated to the intellectual capital of America, Boston, there to continue the offensive. Other liberals at the same time were also doing some organizing, though the results were not integrated nationally and could hardly have aroused the apprehension of the American religious community. By July 1873, however, there were nine local leagues listed in the *Index,* the first having been organized in St. Louis. But of these nine leagues, the one destined to play the most significant role was that of Boston, which was formed under the auspices of the Boston Spiritualists Union. Their organ, the *Banner of Light,* hoped to be a "powerful ally" of the *Index* in these "great and important measures."[6] The Spiritualists had voted unanimously on 18 January to call all Boston liberals to a meeting under the standard of Abbot's "Nine Demands," and on the day following a preliminary meeting was held and committee appointed to prepare a report on the matter. Soon after, this group, which with a few additions became the core of Liberal League activity in Boston, voted to organize.

Transferring the *Index* to Boston brought forth another formal assault on ecclesiasticism, with the immediate goal of revising the Massachusetts laws on the tax exemption of all nonpublic property,

---

[6]*Banner of Light,* 25 January 1873.

including that of churches and educational institutions. "No American citizen has the right to defraud his child of a thorough secular education," Abbot declared, making clear that his educational views ran parallel to his secularism.[7] In November data on tax-exempt property were presented, while on a practical level another great petition was begun, most specifically for the Massachusetts General Court, but also for the U.S. Congress. Furthermore, the "Religious Freedom Amendment" was framed and given a permanent place in the *Index* standing matter as a counter-suggestion to the "Theological Amendment." The amendment (suggested as a substitute for the existing First Amendment) appeared first in the *Index* in 1874. The purpose was to make it impossible for the government to aid any religious group either directly or indirectly and at the same time to assure all citizens complete freedom from any kind of religious test. It was designed to apply at all levels of government, from national to municipal.

These efforts were not entirely in vain. Between 12,000 and 15,000 names were obtained for the Massachusetts petition, which was then submitted by the Hon. Moses Kimball, whereupon a joint special committee was organized in August 1874 to hold public hearings.[8] The committee held seven hearings, at one of which Abbot presented his case. There was also considerable outside discussion of the issue, including many speeches by Abbot; but in most cases the specific issue was clouded and the chances of any action were dimmed by the sweeping implications of Abbot's "Nine Demands." Even to mild Christians these propositions seemed too demonic to deserve confutation.

In 1875 the secularist movement took a new turn in favor of the idea of an integrated national organization. After considerable correspondence, Damon Y. Kilgore, a prominent Spiritualist and one of the leaders of the Philadelphia League, proposed specific arrangements that Abbot accepted in the *Index*.[9] In response the Boston league met, approved the proposals, and named five delegates. In September a formal "Call" for a "national convention," signed by John S. Dye, secretary of the Philadelphia League, was issued.

On the afternoon of 17 September 1875, approximately fifty delegates, representing eight of the existing thirty leagues, were called to order. Abbot was made permanent president and Damon Y. Kil-

---

[7]*Index*, 25 September 1873.

[8]Boston *Daily Globe*, 8 August 1874.

[9]Kilgore to FEA, 26 April 1875; *Index*, 6 May; 29 July 1875.

gore was named secretary. After brief opening remarks and the reading of letters from various "liberals," committees were elected. On the same day, with a dispatch that suggests that "counsels had been ripened beforehand," the full report of the newly elected committee on resolutions was presented. The first six resolutions involved stating and elaborating the goal of "absolute separation of Church and State" and "immediate and absolute secularization of the state." The seventh resolution was a call for a "General Congress" to meet in Philadelphia on or before 4 July 1876. The last one called for hearty cooperation with the German Freie Gemeinde of North America, which Professor Alexander Loos represented. On the following day, all eight resolutions were passed. Two public meetings were also held, with Abbot addressing some 200 people about "The Coming Religion" in the morning and extemporaneously speaking again in the evening regarding the Liberal League movement. Charles C. Burleigh, one of Abbot's few supporters at Syracuse in 1866, followed with a "powerful and unanswerable" critique of the "Theological Amendment."[10]

Abbot returned to Boston inspired, and the *Index* reflected the new emphasis. Despite controversies that served to make many radicals fear that they were threatened by a new John Knox, antiecclesiasticism and especially anti-Catholicism became the dominant notes. Part of the cost of this new vehemence became apparent soon after the Philadelphia meeting when A. W. Stevens, the trusted associate editor, left the *Index* with the reminder that he was "naturally disinclined to organized aggression."[11]

Yet while the *Index* suffered continuing financial losses, the Liberal League seemed to be prospering. Three different funds were established and the returns were surprisingly generous. In May applications for membership were sent to virtually every known liberal in the United States and Canada, and more than eight hundred of them asked for membership. In June between five and six thousand circulars were sent out to every daily and weekly journal in the country telling of the Congress. The *Index* of 15 June published the formal "Call"; the first meeting was to be on 1 July.[12]

---

[10]*Report of the Centennial Congress of Liberals and Organization of the National Liberal League at Philadelphia . . . with an Introduction and Appendix* (Boston, 1876) 23. Hereafter referred to as *N.L.L. Report*. This report contains a brief history of the 1875 meeting.

[11]*Index*, 30 September 1875.

[12]*N.L.L. Report*, 30, 63; *Index*, 6 July 1876.

That the National Reform Association, which was the name of the reorganized "Theological Amendment" organization, was to hold its national convention in Philadelphia at the end of June by no means served to make the occasion less dramatic. Certain other organizations were meeting in the "Centennial City" as well. The American Alliance of American Voters, a nativist group that at least shared Abbot's anti-Catholicism, had convened there in May, and the National Women's Suffrage Association was to meet on 4 July at the First Unitarian Church, where William Henry Furness had now preached for fifty years. More closely related to the Liberal League movement was the Freie Gemeinde, which was scheduled to convene during the last three days of June and then be joined by representatives from the Turn-Associations, the Association for the Propagation of Radical Principles, the Socialist-Democratic Party, and other similar-minded German-speaking organizations. From these they would organize the German Union of Radicals on a platform of secularism, rationalism, "direct democracy," and egalitarianism. They made Professor Loos their delegate to the Congress of Liberals to establish a basis for cooperation.[13]

On Saturday afternoon, 1 July, the Centennial Congress was called to order in Concert Hall; greetings were exchanged, the order of business adopted, and the constitution approved. In the evening permanent organization was effected, the list of twenty-five vice-presidents reviewed, and the officers who had been recommended by the committee on nominations were unanimously elected. The final hour was spent in hearing reports from delegates as to the progress and problems of liberalism in their areas. The following day was an occasion for public meetings. Abbot began this Sunday morning program by reading letters from various distinguished liberals who had indicated their sympathy with the movement, and he spoke on "The Liberal Movement." In the sessions that followed other speakers continued to harp on such issues as antiecclesiasticism, the separation of church and state, and the sufficiency of natural morality. The final session was called to order for the reading of "The Address of the National Liberal League to the People of the United States." This document was an orderly statement of the outlook affirmed in the resolutions. It made the "Religious Freedom Amendment" the focal point of the congress: "Here on the hundredth anniversary of that mighty word, we as solemnly declare the *State's Total Independence of the Church.*

---

[13]See their *Address* in the *N.L.L. Report,* 54-56.

Will you ratify this new word of freedom?"[14] On this note the convention was adjourned *sine die.*

In retrospect the congress seems to have been at least moderately successful. Of the 794 persons invited to the meetings, 172 were present to be enrolled as charter members, and some of them were nationally known figures. Most of these came individually as interested liberals; however, eight local leagues sent a total of twenty-seven delegates, five German organizations sent thirteen delegates, the First Congregation of the Religion of Humanity in New York sent four, and the Investigator Society of Boston, one. These delegates met over a period of four days and in eight sessions, despite weather that made the hall like a furnace, and they dispatched with virtual unanimity a vast amount of business. The addresses, moreover, had been dignified, scholarly, and coordinated; the lessons of the F.R.A. about opening the rostrum to all manner of views had been learned. The likelihood of continued unified action seemed assured by the fact that all of the new Board of Directors (except Kilgore) were Boston men who had long been working together.

The "First Battle Field" of the young league brought no glory though Abbot considered it "a defeat which, like that at Bunker Hill, is a victory in disguise." The issue arose over the decision of the Commission of the Philadelphia Centennial Exposition to close its gates on Sunday. Supported by a petition from 60,000 Philadelphia laborers, the Congress of Liberals formally protested that such a policy was an unwarranted concession to Christianity. The Sabbatarian cause was pleaded by T. P. Stevenson, who threw an "odium theologicum" over the attempt by citing the "Nine Demands of Liberalism."[15]

Abbot found such methods reprehensible, yet he was opposed so unanimously by the religious press that his objections had little effect. Even A. W. Stevens defended Stevenson by pointing out that the "Nine Demands" were, in fact, imbedded in the very constitution of the Liberal League. He upbraided the *Index* for not defending the cause of labor during the recent depression, yet now waxing so eloquent because workers could not go to an exposition on Sundays.[16] In any event, the Christian forces prevailed, and in a vote representing thirty-nine states in the commission, the protest was defeated by

---

[14]Ibid., 169.

[15]*Index*, 20 July; 3 August 1876.

[16]*New Age*, 29 July; 12 August 1876.

nineteen votes. What liberal "victory" their vote "disguises" is difficult to see.

The second battle of the Liberal League was against the proposal
for a sixteenth amendment to the Constitution that came before the
Congress in August 1876. The measure, which prohibited the diversion of public funds to sectarian education, had been first introduced
in December 1871 to Senator William M. Stewart of Nevada. James
G. Blaine introduced a similar measure on 14 December 1875 under
circumstances that suggested a high degree of political opportunism
since his aspirations then centered upon the Republican presidential
nomination.[17] The matter was also adverted to by President Grant in
his annual message; and on 6 August 1876 it was reported by the Judiciary Committee, debated and passed by the Democratic-con-
trolled House. Various amendments and versions of this resolution
were then presented in the Senate by Aaron A. Sargent (California),
Frederick T. Frelinghuysen (New Jersey), and Isaac P. Christiancy
(Michigan), whereupon these versions together with the House resolution were referred to the Senate Judiciary Committee; on 10 August 1876 this body reported its substitute resolution.

The amendment as now framed was substantially different.
Whereas the House resolution applied only to existing school funds
and left enforcement to the states, the Senate version augmented the
powers of Congress and extended the scope of the inhibitions so as to
prevent the diversion of any public funds to sectarian ends. It also included a disclaimer, stating that this could not be construed as pro-
hibiting the "reading of the Bible" in any school or institution. In
addition, the Senate version vowed not to impair the rights of property "already vested." (It guaranteed, in effect, that church property
would not be taxed.)

Despite an immense amount of procedural confusion and uncertainty, the debates made it quite clear that the changes wrought by
the Senate committee had alienated much support and that both its
supporters and critics conceived it to be directed against the Catholic
Church. This seemed to be recognized even by those who opposed it
on grounds of its being an unnecessary invasion of states' rights. When
it came to a vote in an evening session, 14 August 1876, the Senate
split on an almost straight party vote and the measure failed to gain

---

[17]Joint Resolution to H.R. No. 1, *Congressional Record* (44th Congress)
4:205. As to Blaine's motives, see the remarks of Senator William W. Eaton
of Connecticut, ibid., 5592.

the two-thirds support that would have been required for passage.[18] Abbot, of course, rejoiced when a measure favored by the National Reform Association was defeated. He favored the outward intention of the amendment, but he could not sanction the accomplishment of this end at the cost of guaranteeing constitutional protection for the Bible in the schools and ecclesiastical tax-exemption. The threat of its success and subsequent efforts to revive the amendment served, nevertheless, to stimulate Liberal League activity.

Aside from these direct clashes there were other more general tendencies that seemed even more ominous to secularist minds. Abbot was particularly incensed by the way political leaders and aspirants tried to outdo each other in professions of piety, having long since characterized President Grant's statement that the Bible was "the sheet anchor of our liberties" as one of "those popular and melancholy delusions which constitute the darkest cloud of our national future."[19] He now rebuked the president again for proclaiming Thanksgiving Day, pointing out that Jefferson's inaction concerning this "tradition" was more exemplary. During the campaign of 1876, moreover, he saw the "baleful political influence" of Protestantism operating in the Republican party just as Roman Catholicism did among the Democrats. It seemed impossible under the circumstances to bring any kind of Liberal League pressure to bear. When in November the Philadelphia Council refused to accept a bust of Thomas Paine, and with the presidential election still undecided, Abbot called for separate political action: "A third great party is a logical necessity [and] it will yet prove itself to be also an historical necessity."[20]

This conviction grew in urgency, and as the next annual meeting of the N.L.L. drew near, Abbot began laying plans. Robert Ingersoll was asked to accept the nomination for president, and though he made no commitment, he promised to be present (though he never did attend). In the meantime Abbot issued the call for the first annual congress to be held in Rochester, New York, on 26-28 October 1877. He admitted that his previous opposition to political action was ill-advised and so appealed "to all Patriots and Liberals [for] a New Conscience Party" on a tripartite platform: (1) total separation of church and state; (2) "national protection for national citizens," assuring free-

---

[18]Ibid., 4:5580-95.

[19]*Index*, 6 July 1876.

[20]Ibid., 2, 16 November 1876.

dom for all sects and races and equal rights for both women and former slaves; and (3) universal education.[21]

On the morning of 26 October 1877 Abbot called the first session
to order in Corinthian Hall and addressed it with regard to the political needs of the hour. The rest of the day was spent on routine business, resolution framing, and reelecting almost all of the incumbent
officers. On the day following, politics was in the air, with Ingersoll
and Abbot being nominated to a ticket. Yet because the latter de-
clined and since the former was absent, it was decided to postpone
nominations for a year and to concentrate instead on expanding the
Liberal League movement.

Sunday was a day for speeches, and 1,500 people attended the
evening meeting, most likely to hear Elizur Wright, the famous old
abolitionist, speak on "Republican Taxation." Although many of the
big names (including Ingersoll) were absent, Abbot was not disappointed. "Success!" he concluded in his diary; and in the next issue of
the *Index* he congratulated the league on "the singular independence
of great names evinced by this convention."[22]

His optimism was not totally unfounded, since the N.L.L. was to
a certain degree stronger and bigger than it had been a year before.
Twenty leagues now belonged and seventy-nine new individual
members had joined the original one hundred seventy-four on the
charter list. Though the treasury was hardly swelling (only $455.10
had had to be accounted for at Rochester), new activities revitalized
the movement after the turn of the new year. In January 1878 Senator George F. Edmunds introduced the "Theological Amendment"
again, giving rise to a new series of *Index* editorials and another petition that garnered 10,660 names. Having noted that the Republicans had previously supported the measure while Democrats opposed
it on a straight party vote, Abbot discovered that Democrats could be
useful notwithstanding their league with "Romanism and Rebellion";
Senator Thomas F. Bayard, a Delaware Democrat, submitted the new
petition.[23] Such interest even made it possible to revive the flagging
First Boston Liberal League, and after a reorganization meeting at
Mrs. Theodore Parker's in February, Minot J. Savage consented to

---

[21]"Wanted—A New Conscience-Party," ibid., 27 September 1877.

[22]For a copy of Wright's "Address," see *Index*, 15 November 1877. For
accounts of the convention, see ibid., 8 November 1877; and Diary.

[23]*Index*, 31 January; 28 February 1878.

be president. He took office with a new slate of officers and a revised constitution in March.

The most crucial development in the months between the first and second annual congresses, however, was the rise of a new and divisive issue in the Liberal League movement. Its origins were diverse and ultimately revolved around two problems: (1) censorship of the mails in the interest of reducing traffic in obscene and blasphemous literature and (2) the challenge offered by the "free love element" to American mores and morals, since much of their literature was ruled to be either obscene or blasphemous. They were problems, coming events would show, that could not be solved within the framework of the National Liberal League.

CHAPTER EIGHT

OBSCENITY, FREE LOVE, AND THE COLLAPSE OF THE LEAGUE

OBSCENITY WAS AN OLD PROBLEM, and in America as elsewhere legal action had been taken against it. Connecticut and Massachusetts statutes dated at least to 1834 and 1835, while federal action had been taken shortly thereafter. In 1842 the importation of indecent pictures and articles was prohibited; the measure was tightened by an amendment in 1857; and in 1865 the transmission of obscene books and pictures through the mail had been prohibited. A bill of similar intent was passed by the New York legislature in 1868, but in Boss Tweed's, New York, the proscribed matter was still for sale on the newsstands. There were many people who demanded new efforts to eliminate this "deadly poison, cast into the fountain of moral purity."[1] The New York Y.M.C.A. was prominent in the efforts at suppression, but the organization of a systematic assault awaited the zeal and energy of a Brooklyn dry-goods dealer, born of rigorously orthodox parents in 1844 on a farm near New Canaan, Connecticut.

Anthony Comstock became involved in the "cause" in June 1871, through a successful conflict about a saloon near his place of business that was violating Sabbath law. Early in the following year Morris K. Jessup of the Y.M.C.A. gave the first financial support ($650) to Comstock's larger war on obscene literature. William Haynes, an Irish surgeon turned publisher who committed suicide before he was apprehended, was the first victim, but others followed. In two more years the small group of men who constituted the Committee for the Suppression of Vice of the New York Y.M.C.A. were to expend nearly $10,000 in similar efforts.[2]

Two sensational sisters, Victoria C. Woodhull and Tennessee Claflin, provided the occasion for an arrest that propelled Comstock

---

[1]A statement by Anthony Comstock quoted in Heywood Broun and Margaret Leech, *Anthony Comstock: Roundsman of the Lord* (New York: Literary Guild, 1927) 80.

[2]Ibid., 85.

into the public eye. Previously they had operated a cure-all sanitarium in Indiana, but upon coming to New York they established a brokerage office and founded the "radical reformatory paper," *Woodhull and Claflin's Weekly,* which had financial support, it was said, from Cornelius Vanderbilt. In 1871-1872 Victoria was president of the National Association of Spiritualists; in 1872 she was nominated by a New York reformer's convention as the presidential candidate of the Equal Rights party, and she had presented the case of the Women's Rights Association to the House Judiciary Committee.

Shortly after these events it became known that she was practicing her own emancipated "free love gospel" by having Dr. Woodhull, her former husband whom she had married at fourteen and divorced at twenty-eight, living in her home in addition to her present husband, Colonel James H. Blood. In return for the mounting criticism, she unleashed one of the more sensational charges ever to rock the American ecclesiastical world. In the 2 November 1872 issue of her erratic weekly (the previous issue had been published in June), she accused Henry Ward Beecher of illicit relations with the wife of Theodore Tilton, a liberal religious editor. She more or less approved of Beecher's actions but denounced his hypocrisy.

On the basis of an 1872 federal statute against mailing obscene periodicals, Comstock arrested the women, denied bail, and allowed them to languish for a month in the Ludlow Street jail. Despite the efforts and financial aid of that eccentric reformer, George Francis Train, they were finally brought into federal court on 27 January 1873. The publicity of the trials of the two sisters and of Train, combined as it was with the Beecher scandal, proved to be an immense boon to Comstock; but the case was dismissed by the judge's ruling that the 1872 law did not apply to newspapers.[3]

Comstock got the law changed. Working first through Representative Clinton L. Merriam and Senator William A. Buckingham (the ex-war governor of Connecticut), and with the aid of General Benjamin Butler, Senators Windom of Minnesota and Edmunds of Vermont, and despite the diversions offered by the Credit Mobilier

---

[3]For recent discussions of the significance of Woodhull and the "Free Love" movement, see Emanie Louise Sachs, *"The Terrible Siren": Victoria Woodhull, 1838-1927* (New York: Harper and Bros., 1928); Johanna Johnston, *Mrs. Satan: The Incredible Saga of Victoria C. Woodhull* (New York: Putnam, 1967); and M. M. Marberry, *Vicky: A Biography of Victoria C. Woodhull* (New York: Funk and Wagnalls, 1967).

scandal, he obtained (3 March 1873) the signature of President Grant on a new and more comprehensive measure.

Due to Windom's insistence, Comstock was invested as special agent of the Post Office to aid in the enforcement of the measure, and he was later made inspector. That fall Comstock severed all connections with his dry-goods business and shortly thereafter was instrumental in founding, as an organization separate from the Y.M.C.A., the Society for the Suppression of Vice. At this time the old committee reported that through the efforts of Comstock 134,000 pounds of literature, 194,000 photographs, 14,200 pounds of stereotype plates, 60,300 "rubber articles," 5,500 indecent playing cards, and 3,150 boxes of pills and powders had been seized and destroyed, while sentences totaling twenty-four years had been obtained. By 1878 he boasted that his arrests or threats had led fifteen evildoers to suicide. He had designated 165 "obscene" publications when he began his labors, and by 1876 he had destroyed all but five of them. There seemed little left to do, and the annual reports of the society showed a diminishing volume of destruction.[4]

Around 1 May 1878 (a month after Madame Restell, a Fifth Avenue abortionist, had committed suicide after being arrested and committed to prison at Comstock's hands), the crusader spoke in Boston to a group interested in organizing a Boston Society modeled on his. At this meeting in the Park Street Church, which Abbot attended, Comstock admitted to signing false names (even a woman's name), writing decoy letters, and posing as a buyer of illicit commodities.[5] These procedures, which seemed questionable to many, tended to build up resistance to his antivice campaign; but even more effective in arousing opposition were his increasingly virulent attacks on the publishers of what he considered "blasphemous" literature, which could by no stretch of the imagination be called "obscene" even when it was crude and antireligious.

This had been the situation even in 1876 when the matter was broached at the Centennial Congress of Liberals by Stephen Pearl Andrews. Andrews had proposed a twofold resolution that pointed to evidences of "ecclesiastical despotism" and recommended "utmost

---

[4]Broun and Leech, *Comstock,* 152-53. By 1880 Comstock claimed 24 tons of confiscated matter and 450 arrests. Anthony Comstock, *Frauds Exposed* (New York, 1880) 432.

[5]See Abbot's description of the meeting: "The Two Sides of the Shield," *Index,* 13 June 1878.

vigilance" with a view to repealing or drastically revising the 1873 legislation.[6] He also pointed out that one friend of his, John A. Lant, was "lying in a penitentiary" and that another, Dr. E. B. Foote, editor of *Medical Common Sense,* had been on trial. He claimed that Comstock had obtained more than 600 convictions in the past two years. B. F. Underwood and Edward S. Wheeler of Philadelphia were Andrews's chief supporters in this effort; but the Congress, largely influenced by Abbot's friends—Potter, David H. Clark, and C. D. B. Mills (of whom the latter two were also associates with Abbot on the *Index*)—voted to refer the matter to the board of directors for further study and reporting to the next annual meeting. Just before the adjournment of the final session, however, Underwood, who was on the Resolutions Committee, reported two revised resolutions that stated the case against "Comstockery" more briefly and moderately.

The first one recognized the need for dealing with the problems of obscenity, but demanded "that all laws against obscenity and indecency shall be so clear and explicit that none but actual offenders against the recognized principles of purity shall be liable to suffer therein." The second resolution was more closely related to the activities of Comstock.

> Resolved: That we cannot but regard the appointment and authorization by the government of a single individual to inspect our mails, with power to exclude therefrom whatever he deems objectionable, as a delegation of authority dangerous to public and personal liberty, and utterly inconsistent with the genius of free institutions.

These resolutions were passed. On this fateful issue, therefore, the N.L.L. was committed to a policy of "reform" but *not* "repeal." The difference was to become crucial.[7]

Abbot was in complete accord with the position taken by the Congress of Liberals; and although it did not become a major matter in the *Index* there were, during the ensuing year, frequent attacks on indiscriminate use of the new power of censorship lodged with the Post Office Department and its inspector. One of the earliest of these came in the summer of 1877 when Annie Besant, a frequent English secularist contributor to the *Index* (and later to be a leader in the Theosophical movement), and Charles Bradlaugh, a leader of the English secularist movement and an outspoken atheist, were indicted in En-

---

[6]*N.L.L. Report,* 1876, 157ff.

[7]Ibid., 157-62, 170-71.

gland for publishing *The Fruits of Philosophy* by Dr. Charles Knowlton because the book contained information on reproduction and contraception that was seen as deleterious to morals. Abbot agreed that the book was immoral, since it could encourage immorality, especially among youth, but he did not think this justified prosecution.[8] Later in the year, however, there were two arrests by Comstock that brought the issue much closer to home.

Ezra Harvey Heywood of Princeton, Massachusetts, was an old follower of Theodore Parker regarding both antislavery and theology. He was also a pacifist, reformer, and advocate of free love. He published his own little magazine (the *Word*), organized the New England Free Love League in 1873, and published a pamphlet, *Cupid's Yoke: Or the Binding Forces of Conjugal Life,* which set forth his views on love, freedom, and marriage. In November 1877 he was arrested while lecturing in Boston. Abbot believed that Heywood had written his pamphlet

> to advocate what he himself positively believed to be a higher and not a lower morality. Although his "free love" theory of morals . . . is one which we just as positively believe to be false, one-sided, logically ridiculous, and morally mischievous in all its tendencies, nevertheless we concede his full and entire right to plead his case as best he can before the public.[9]

He therefore protested when Heywood was hauled into the U.S. District Court, sentenced on 25 June 1878 to two years and $100 fine, and thrown into the Dedham jail where he remained until he received a presidential pardon late in the year.

From his position on the Heywood case Abbot never withdrew, but in frequent editorials he clarified his stand, explaining that there were three categories of writing: inflammatory obscenity, "intellectually addressed matter" on any subject, and material that only incidentally used techniques or passages that out of context could be considered obscene. He stated that the first type should be prohibited, that the second should not, and that the third was questionable. Heywood he put in class three and advocated no prosecution since "its departures from decency are rather in its suggestions than in its expression."[10] Abbot made it perfectly clear at the same time that he

---

[8]*Index,* 28 June 1877.

[9]Ibid., 6 December 1877.

[10]"The Heywood Case, and the Principles It Involves," *Index,* 4 July 1878.

disagreed utterly with Heywood's own concept of "personal sover-
eignty," which made even taxation and law enforcement impossible.
In a long series of editorials he also clarified other aspects of the problem: that Comstock did *not* open first-class mail, that other classes of
mail had never been considered inviolable, and that the Supreme
Court of the United States had ruled without dissent that the Comstock laws were constitutional.[11]

November 1877 had also seen the arrest of D. M. Bennett, the
publisher of the radical, freethinking *Truth-Seeker* of New York, for
his publication of two tracts: "An Open Letter to Jesus Christ" and an
essay on the reproduction of marsupials. Through the intercession of
Robert Ingersoll, this case was dismissed without trial; but Comstock
continued to hound the outspoken "truth-seeker" and ultimately
brought him to trial in March 1879 for having sent copies of *Cupid's
Yoke* through the mails. Bennett was convicted and sentenced to thirteen months' imprisonment by a U.S. Circuit Court.[12]

By this time Abbot and Bennett had divided violently and beyond reconciliation for reasons that lay in their differing reactions to
Comstock's activity. Abbot insisted that only *reform* of existing laws
was necessary, whereas Bennett insisted on outright *repeal*. The rift
began to widen within a month after Bennett's first arrest when the
Truth-Seeker began assembling an immense petition to Congress demanding an end to the Comstock laws. Though no less a man than Ingersoll headed the list of signers, Abbot decided at the outset that "a
great danger threatens the liberal movement at this time." Far from
signing the petition, he declared that "Anthony Comstock has done a
great deal of dirty but most necessary work." He opposed absolutely
Bennett's demand that antiobscenity authority be vested with the
states and territories, even though he had received a letter saying that
Comstock was plotting to outlaw the *Investigator,* then the *Index,* and
finally the works of Mill, Spencer, and Darwin.[13]

Concerning these issues Abbot met all comers and "libertinism
versus liberalism" became the dominant theme of the *Index*, with
every issue containing contributions, letters, and replies to letters on
the subject. Not all of his contributors were in agreement, however.
Elizur Wright was especially outspoken in his support of Bennett. But

---

[11]"Inviolability of the Mails," *Index*, 17 January 1878; "The Two Sides
of the Shield," ibid., 13 June 1878.

[12]Broun and Leech, *Comstock*, 175-81.

[13]"Freedom the Friend of Purity," *Index*, 20 December 1877.

Albert Warren Kelsey of St. Louis, the most recent addition to the list of editorial contributors, spoke for the majority of them when he objected to the "chartering of Libertinism" and observed, "Anthony Comstock may be an evil; but the evidence shows him to be a necessary one."[14]

General Benjamin Butler (in sharp reversal of his earlier support of Comstock) presented the Bennett petition for repeal of the 1873 law in Congress, and in March 1878 hearings before the House Committee on the revision of the laws were scheduled. By June it was clear that the attempt to gain repeal was unsuccessful. One of the devices Comstock used to defend "his" laws was to point out the illicit nature of the endorsements that Bennett had used in the circular prepared to advertise the petition. Abbot had emphasized one of these instances: the case of McKesson and Robbins, a pharmaceutical firm that reported to Abbot in a letter that it had not given its permission for the endorsement's use. The *Truth-Seeker* replied to this irrefutable evidence with a storm of abuse, and launched a counter-charge that Abbot had forged O. B. Frothingham's name in an *Index* publication. The *Truth-Seeker* refused to publish Frothingham's denial of these charges, and though that genial preacher urged Abbot to settle the matter by suing Bennett for libel, he finally consented to write a letter of exoneration that could be printed in the *Index*.[15]

With these two charges against Bennett the enmity between the two men was irrevocably established, and in liberal circles generally the situation continued to become even more strained. On 1 August 1878 came the Faneuil Hall protest meeting about the Heywood imprisonment. Six thousand people crowded to hear various parts of the long series of speeches. Something of the festive air that clung traditionally to this anniversary of the West Indian Slave Emancipation pervaded the scene. But Abbot found the "repeal" sentiment too strong and pronounced the overall result "melancholy." He lamented particularly that Thaddeus Burr Wakeman, a prominent New York "repealer," had repeated his elaborate arguments for the unconstitutionality of the Comstock laws despite the unanimous decision of the Supreme Court.[16]

---

[14]"Shall We Charter Libertinism?" *Index*, 21 February 1878.

[15]*Truth-Seeker,* 6 July 1878; *Index,* 25 July 1878; Diary, 11, 15 March; 5 April 1878.

[16]Diary, 1 August 1878.

Relations were further exacerbated at a four-day Freethinkers' Convention held in Watkins, New York, in August of the same year. This affair was "called" by Dr. T. L. Brown, president of the Freethinkers' Association of Western New York, and arranged by H. L. Green of Salamanca, who had been Abbot's main aide in staging the Rochester Congress of 1877. By and large, even Abbot admitted that the convention was a success. For four days five to six hundred interested people had attended meetings and heard addresses by a number of eminent liberals. But discordant notes were struck. C. D. B. Mills had warned of the rising strength of the "repeal element," claiming that it was becoming more closely allied with a growing body of people interested in "free love." Abbot was naturally alarmed that one of the fifteen resolutions passed at Watkins pledged the group "to advance sexual purity," a term often having connotations of free love. He was disgusted that liberalism was further identified with libertinism when Bennett and two others were arrested by local authorities for selling publicly the memorable treatise of Ezra Heywood.

These were troubled times for Abbot. To the already burning issue of "repeal versus reform" was added the serious possibility that the "free love forces" would capture the whole National Liberal League!

Recent scholarship has noted that despite the relatively chaste nature of the postbellum Free-Love movement, it nonetheless touched a tender nerve in the American Victorian consciousness, and Abbot was no exception. His views on the subject, as on most others, had assumed definitive shape early and seemed unlikely to change. More than a year earlier he had denounced the "notorious" Oneida community for its views on "complex marriage."[17] He saw a "fatal disorder" in the offing. In issuing the call for the 1878 congress, therefore, he had announced his readiness for combat. To head it off the incumbent officers announced their candidacy for reelection on a platform demanding retention of the Comstock laws. Reprinting the debates regarding the "Underwood Resolutions" at the Centennial Congress, Abbot made his position clear in an editorial: "[W]e have received information that a secret movement is on foot to surprise and capture the National Liberal League at its next Annual Congress for the purpose of making it reverse its record, and come out in favor of the *total repeal* of the obscene literature laws as opposed to their *radical reform*."[18]

---

[17]*Index*, 28 June 1877.

[18]"Public Discussion vs. Secret Plots," ibid., 19 September 1878.

The issue stirred up a hornet's nest. T. B. Wakeman, the "great legal expert" of the "repealers," replied *in extenso* (only to have Abbot point out "three evasions and five men of straw" in an accompanying editorial). Ezra Heywood, writing from the Dedham jail, demanded a clean, consistent abolition of the laws. The *Truth-Seeker* fulminated, and Benjamin R. Tucker, editing Heywood's paper, the *Word,* urged "immediate, unconditional, and permanent repeal of all laws against obscenity, whether Municipal, State or National."[19] Clearly, the upcoming congress of the Liberal League would find it difficult to avoid the question.

Before he boarded a train for the 1878 congress, Abbot confided his deepest fears to his diary: "How strange that I should be called to fight the second greatest battle of my life at *Syracuse!* Will it be a second defeat? Or will the defeat prove in fact, as before, a second victory? I go with as high a purpose as in 1866. I cannot be defeated."[20] He was not defeated. Looking over the shambles of the N.L.L. in the first issue of the *Index* after the Syracuse Congress (31 October), he pronounced it a "VICTORY!"

Abbot arrived in Syracuse a day in advance, using the time to make last-minute preparations. At ten o'clock on the following day 138 delegates and members opened the congress with Abbot in the chair, but the whole first morning was lost in a parliamentary tangle, the most crucial result of which was the defeat of the established order-of-business by a clique headed by T. B. Wakeman and Asa K. Butts, aided by a miscount on the final vote. Only after much haranguing did they elect a "general committee" with a subcommittee on resolutions, nominations, and membership.[21]

At the second session, in the afternoon, the conflict was transferred to the oratorical level. Wakeman repeated his Faneuil Hall speech on the unconstitutionality of the Comstock laws, and Judge E. P. Hurlbut of Albany—one of the league's vice-presidents—answered with a legislative proposal that would both be effective against obscenity and protect the rights of free speech and press. But when Courtlandt Palmer, who realized that the "reformers" controlled the subcommittee, moved that the body-at-large *instruct* them to report

---

[19]See ibid., 17, 24 October 1878; S. P. Putnam, *Four Hundred Years of Free Thought* (New York, 1894) 819ff.

[20]Diary, 21 October 1878.

[21]*Index,* 31 October 1878, is the main source of information regarding this congress.

a resolution in favor of repeal, he stirred up arguments that ran on into the next session. The debate continued until 11:00 P.M., when Abbot finally ruled that an ambiguous resolution offered by Dr. E. B. Foote, Jr. referred *all* of the scattered amendments to committee. This was passed and no objections were raised.

On the Sabbath morning the rancor of the parties only seemed to increase. Accusations of bribery were made and ruled out of order; wrangling followed. With matters at an impasse, Palmer presented the compromise proposal of the resolutions subcommittee. It applauded freedom, opposed obscenity, and postponed judgment on the Comstock laws until the following year. Wakeman yielded "reluctantly" to this position and Abbot gained passage for the motion by pointing out that the league was, in fact, already committed to the "reform" position by the 1876 resolutions. During the remainder of the morning other resolutions were passed and the Directors' and the Treasurer's reports were made and accepted. For the elections in the afternoon, as Abbot remarks in his diary, "the mask was dropped" and the "repealers" had their day.

The nominations subcommittee rendered a divided report, with three members proposing the incumbents and two members proposing a group of persons known or believed to be strongly in favor of "repeal." Asa K. Butts passed a motion limiting debate, and in the ballot for president, Abbot was defeated 76 to 51, at which point he left the rostrum and took a seat in the auditorium while Vice-President Brown took the gavel. But before further business could be transacted, Hurlbut offered his resignation and strode from the hall, followed shortly by Hallowell and Underwood. At this juncture E. E. Gordon stood up and proposed that all those who were of a similar mind should withdraw. "This spontaneous, impressive, solemn movement of the minority was a great and unexpected moral protest, which filled us with awe and imperatively commanded our adhesion," Abbot later wrote.[22] The Syracuse *Daily Standard* used a different kind of language. "Their [the repealers'] remarks sometimes almost polluted the atmosphere of the opera house, and one who said that 'if they should be left alone, they would stink themselves to death' was not so far out of the way as he might have been. The decent element was compelled to leave."[23]

---

[22]Ibid.

[23]Syracuse *Daily Standard*, 28 October 1878.

The righteous minority moved to the Syracuse House where Gordon called them to order. Judge Hurlbut was made chairman and a committee of five was appointed to prepare a statement. An hour later the group reconvened to hear the report, which said, in effect, that the election was a "breach of faith." That night the thirty-four "reformers" decided to adopt the old constitution, stand on the principles of 1876, and take a new name, The National Liberal League of America. Abbot (who had absented himself) was told that Judge Hurlbut's speech nominating him to be the "new" president "was the most eloquent and pathetic they had ever heard, drawing tears from many." Though such forceful words may not have been necessary, all the old officers were elected. They also called local organizations to their standard, voting to accept all charters as valid; but the treasury and roster of leagues remained with the old N.L.L.[24]

On Monday there were various exchanges between groups and attempts at reunion. Wakeman and Underwood conferred without success, and the former spoke to Abbot only to be sharply dismissed: "You have chosen your own course. Now you must take the consequences." Upon being told that he had misapprehended the motives of the "repealers," Abbot shot back: "I have *not* misapprehended; I apprehend you perfectly; I have nothing to say to you."[25]

In such spirits the delegates returned home, and the *Index* took up the controversy, announcing with somewhat forced optimism that "the old flag flies triumphant" and that liberalism is better off without this "disaffected and vindictive clique." The weeks that followed were a time of readjustment. Certain members that had been elected as officers in both groups affirmed their final allegiance. Around the election of Elizur Wright to the presidency of the N.L.L. a separate controversy arose. Abbot had suggested at the outset that he felt no desire to impugn that aged fighter for justice. He is "one of our best and most honored personal friends," he wrote, "and had he been at Syracuse, he would have been disgusted at the spirit, tactics, and proceedings of those who used his name without authority." But in this Abbot was mistaken, for Wright not only took the office but dealt out hard words for the N.L.L.A.: "With highest respect for their motives, it seems to me that the minority of the Congress, in seceding from the majority and forming another League, have rather unwittingly seceded from the principle of secularism, in the direction of becoming

---

[24]Diary, 28 October 1878.

[25]Ibid.

a church." He went on to express his doubts about Hurlbut's proposals and stated that obscenity should be attacked through means less dangerous to liberty. Later he declared that the league of which he was president was "*not* irrevocably committed . . . to repeal" and that the way remained open for voting on this question of policy at the next annual meeting.[26]

Underwood meanwhile used his editorial privileges in the *Index* to point out that men such as Wakeman, Parton, and Wright were by no means "free lovers," that the whole obscenity question should be dropped, and that the two leagues should unite in the following year under their true secularist standard. Abbot, however, was adamant on this issue and ever remained so. "As to 'reunion,' " he answered, "we have but one word to speak. . . . The only 'reunion' which we shall sanction will be unequivocally, avowedly, and emphatically on the platform of 'reform.' " He said that if the N.L.L.A. reunited on any other basis, he would stay behind.[27]

However sanguine Abbot's hopes were—or however certain of general support—there was still no flocking to his standard. One of the saddest blows was the "desertion" of O. B. Frothingham, who had written that he thought an alien issue had riven the vital cause. This had "alienated his sympathy" until such time as "harmony be restored." The returns of voting in the local leagues were hardly more heartening. Florence, led by David H. Clark, was the first to change banners, and slowly a few others followed suit. In a big meeting on 15 December the First Boston League moved for the N.L.L.A., and at the same meeting the Honorable Samuel E. Sewall informed all present that he was resigning as a vice-president of the N.L.L. By the end of 1878 three others, where prominent "reform" leaders were influential, had followed suit: Syracuse, Albany, and Passaic City. A year later the list had been augmented by Jacksonville, Illinois, Rochester, New York, and Chelsea, Massachusetts. Beyond these areas the N.L.L.A. never went, and in December 1879 it was voted inexpedient to hold an annual congress. At this same time, because "the name 'National Liberal League' has become so widely and injuriously associated in the public mind with attempts to repeal the postal law," it was voted (and ultimately passed by the approval of the locals) that their name be changed to the "American Liberal Union."

---

[26]*Index,* 21 November 1878; 20 March 1879.

[27]Ibid., 12 December 1878.

As an organization it ceased to exist except insofar as the *Index* kept up a running attack on the N.L.L., its activities and members.[28]

The old N.L.L. fared better—though not because of the press it received in the *Index!* A year later it held its first congress without Abbot in Cincinnati, not only proving its own vitality but spawning a political party as well. Meeting as the N.L.L., it officially expressed its objections to Bennett's conviction and adopted resolutions written by Ingersoll with regard to the obscenity question, disapproving of regulation by the Postal Department "until the Christian world expunge from the so-called 'sacred' Bible every passage that cannot be read without covering the check of modesty with the blush of shame."[29]

The body thereafter converted itself into the "National Liberty Party," approved all the resolutions of the league, and presented an immense platform that included almost every plank dear to American reformers' hearts and beyond—even to the point of equal distribution of the "products of labor." Child labor, land policy, currency laws, and the electoral college were singled out for reform, as were Sabbath and sumptuary laws. Abbot called it socialistic, but what he abhorred most was a statement on women's rights that departed from traditional suffragette diction: "The reform by which woman shall be politically and practically emancipated, and be given the control of herself and her destiny." There is some indication of political activity along these lines but nothing to indicate that the new party made any dent whatsoever in the election of 1880.[30]

The N.L.L. itself continued to grow after 1878. There were 162 locals represented at Cincinnati and 225 at the 1880 meeting in Chicago, where Wakeman was elected to succeed Wright as president. At the eighth annual congress its name was changed to the American Secular Union with Robert Ingersoll as president, and the organization remained active at least down to the end of the century. Abbot developed other interests long before then, but during the two years after the Syracuse meeting, he pursued a program of exposure and vilification that almost defies exaggeration.

Whereas from December 1878 to March 1879 the *Index* had featured much academic discussion of the Comstock question, it now became increasingly devoted to furious personal attacks. Ever since the

---

[28]Diary, 19 November; 15 December 1878.

[29]"The Cincinnati Meeting," *Index*, 2 October 1879.

[30]Charles J. Harbold, *The National Liberal League: What It Is and What It Is Not* (Cincinnati, 1880) passim.

rise of these challengers to his leadership of the N.L.L., Abbot had been emphasizing with increasing vigor the need to judge leaders by their character. The theoretical aspects of this problem were not neglected, but with Abbot it was not a philosophical matter. He began exposing the moral corruption of the opposition leaders, revealing the "abyss of shame" into which they had cast the liberal movement.

Abbot centered his attack on Bennett and A. L. Rawson, secretary of the N.L.L., in a series of articles. On 30 October 1879 Abbot reprinted a long exposé first published by the (Chicago, Spiritualist) *Religio-Philosophical Journal*, which had printed letters proving that Bennett had been having adulterous relations with a young girl.[31] This was accompanied by further facts on the Rawson case that indicated beyond reasonable doubt that he had in the past not been entirely circumspect in his marital duties, having in fact married a second time without divorcing his first wife. Five thousand copies of this *Index* were published and sent to virtually every press and periodical in the nation.[32]

Abbot also carried his attack across the Atlantic and addressed an open letter to Charles Bradlaugh, imploring him to realize that the American secularists with whom he was dealing were morally corrupt. Later he printed Bradlaugh's unexcited reply and accompanied it with further evidence on Rawson, going on to remark that apparently the National [British] Secular Society was of the N.L.L. type, leaning towards pseudoscience and free love. He indicated his preference for the British Secular Union, which was represented by George Jacob Holyoake and others.[33] "Liberals" and "Libertines" (to use Abbot's terms) were never finally able to be reconciled.

In view of its short and tumultuous life, the Liberal League is difficult to assess either as to its impact or its meaning. The most direct influence came to be on Abbot's own thought, for he was forced to overhaul his metaphysical views to cope with the assaults of enemies and to justify the course he steered for the faction that remained loyal to him. In a larger sense, the movement serves to indicate the place and status of religion in the United States in the 1870s. In the almost boyish braggadocio of these secularists, one sees how daring, how unconventional, how dangerously radical they thought themselves to be. Yet on the reverse side of this phenomenon is the wide popular basis

---

[31]"Another Imposter Unearthed," *Index*, 30 October 1879. The letter had already convinced President Hayes that a pardon was unwarranted.

[32]Comstock reprinted most of these findings in *Frauds Exposed*, 443ff.

[33]*Index*, 13 November 1879.

of Christianity and the traditional morality that it strengthened and justified. In any extreme circumstance the greater number of Universalists, Unitarians, and other Christian liberals referred to the majority view for their standards: presidents and senators were as much subjects as products of this immense force.

Abbot, the *Index,* and the Liberal Leagues demonstrate as well the immense capacity of American thinkers to divorce their speculations on ethics, religion, and even politics from social and economic realities. It is hard to realize, for instance, the degree to which the religious press—conservative, liberal, or radical—could ignore the practical issues of the nation, yet it is only against this background that the early preachers of the social gospel can be awarded their due as revolutionaries.

In terms of influence the league probably affected most people in a negative way. It awakened the churches and the clergy to the challenge of secularism. Abbot's bitter rival in the National Reform Association, the Reverend Huntington Lyman, was correct: the Liberal League was doing for Christianity what Calhoun, Buchanan, and Cass had done for abolitionism. He urged Christians to encourage the leagues. "If it be possible, get them to hold quarterly meetings. They do good every time. The last thing to do is to be afraid of them." Though Abbot became their bête noire, orthodox editors praised him for laying bare with such logical and unsentimental rigor the implications of abandoning the Christian confession.[34]

The positive influence of the league movement was very restricted. The "Nine Demands" frightened moderate reformers. The early alliance with "vulgar" journals such as the *Investigator* and the *Truth-Seeker* alienated "respectable" elements while the later campaign to discredit the "libertines" merely confirmed the general view that atheists, materialists, and freethinkers were a vile, reprehensible lot. The movement, moreover, did not provide a popular religious rationale; like the *Index,* it was essentially destructive in temper. Its adherents agreed on secularism but little else. Reform movements and social work provided a more satisfactory outlet for persons no longer interested in the historical Christian affirmation.

This history also reveals that the radicalism of Abbot's "party" was not nearly as sweeping as he sometimes thought it to be. He and the men who followed him out of the N.L.L., not to mention the far larger group of liberals that never had the temerity to join either or-

---

[34]*Christian Statesman,* 8 November 1877.

ganization, seemed to believe positively what Elizur Wright had implied pejoratively: that they were a church. They accepted the idea of religion; they insisted that morals had a transcendental reference of some sort. They could not cooperate with those who allowed a more thoroughgoing and individualistic naturalism or skepticism to undermine all of the traditional sanctions of life and worship.

In a personal way Abbot proved to be the Anthony Comstock of Free Religion, and the similarity was not merely one of temperament. In 1880 when Comstock wrote his most inclusive apologia—*Frauds Exposed*—Abbot read the book, even those sections showing "Infidelity Wedded to Obscenity," with deep satisfaction. "How gladly would I have shielded them from the shame they have incurred too justly." In 1881 Abbot found it easier to speak with Comstock than with O. B. Frothingham. Each in his way was a "roundsman of the Lord."[35]

---

[35]Diary, 21 January; 23, 30 April; 15 November 1881.

CHAPTER NINE

PRIVATE LIFE IN BOSTON

ABBOT'S INVOLVEMENT in the National Liberal League, and the general intensification of his anti-Christianity during the decade of the 1870s, led to an increased strain in the relationship between him and the Free Religious Association. From his perspective the F.R.A. seemed unable to cut the moorings holding it to the past. On the most obvious level, he was never satisfied or at ease in the F.R.A. because he was a radical anti-Christian in an association of moderate individuals, many of whom were still formally within Unitarian ranks. At annual meetings he regularly asked for absolute opposition to Christianity or any other of the "various historical religions." Many found themselves, however, uneasy with his anti-Christianity, fearing that it was in fact a mask for radical secularism—a charge Abbot would refute by claiming that opposition to Christianity no more implied opposition to religion than did opposition to a panther imply opposition to living protoplasm.

But perhaps even more troublesome was Abbot's increasing attacks upon intuitionalism. As we have seen, intuitionalism to him was the antithesis of scientific method. He went on to explain his position in a series of articles on "scientific ethics." There he assaulted the idea of both "moral sense" and "*a priori* truths." He noted that at present there were three schools of ethics: utilitarian, intuitional, and scientific. The second, or "sentimental," was then in the ascendance in the F.R.A., yet neither of the first two could ultimately be justified. If the weakness of intuitionalism was its abandonment of science, the weakness of the utilitarian school was that it limited moral considerations to the consequences as revealed a posteriori by experience, and denied any intrinsic moral nature to actions. True ethics could only be based on "universal reason" and the "consensus of the competent."

Yet Abbot's rejection of intuitionalism did not go unchallenged. In 1877, for example, he returned to these themes in his Horticultural Hall address on "The Scientific Method in Religion," where he argued that the F.R.A. constitution committed the organization to "scientific theology." "I maintain," he explained, "that its constitution unmistakably defines this reform as consistency in the substitution of the scientific method for the method of authority in religion."[1] In response, Thomas W. Higginson, the old antislavery advocate, published an editorial in the Boston *Commonwealth* in which he accused Abbot of "reading out" of the association men such as Max Müller, W. C. Gannett, and many others. "He sacrifices at a blow that noble comprehensiveness which has been the glory of the Free Religious Association." He also charged that Abbot so emphasized the phrase "to encourage the scientific study of man's religious nature and history," that he ignored the other expressed objects of the F.R.A., such as to "promote . . . pure religion [and] to increase fellowship in the spirit."[2]

Perhaps a formal alienation was inevitable. The break finally did come in 1880, during a period of reorganization in the F.R.A. Abbot, remembering his experience with the Liberal League, wanted strong local organizations but under strict surveillance; however, his plan was rejected. By the summer of 1880, the rift between Abbot and the F.R.A., which had been widening since 1868, had become permanent.

A rift with the F.R.A., though, also meant a rift with the *Index*, which had finally—in July of 1880—come together with the F.R.A. They came together, however, without Abbot. For several years he had worked for this arrangement, and in early May 1880 the *Index* announced that the transaction had been completed. Abbot was bitter. "Not a word of regret was said on the platform of the F.R.A. at the annual convention, as to my leaving the *Index*. I cannot even recall a hint of any such feeling." To Potter he was more explicit:

> The simple truth is that the F.R.A. has shown a degree of stolid unconsciousness of obligation, of moral insensibility and ingratitude for favors received from the Index Association which I never saw equaled except in the case of the N.L.L. . . . It never so much as thanked the Index Association all these ten years, for giving it gratuitous advertizing [*sic*] to the extent of thousands of dollars.[3]

Meanwhile, Boston and Cambridge revealed no less hostility to Abbot's views than other places, and the acrimony became even more painful in the context of old associations and institutions. "There is a

---

[1]Delivered 11 March; published *Index*, 22 March 1877. See also, "Ethics as the Science of Society," ibid., 16 January 1879, and "Three Schools of Ethics," ibid., 9 January 1879.

[2]*Commonwealth*, 31 March 1877.

[3]FEA to Potter, 16 June 1880. See also Diary, 30 May 1880.

social hunger in my heart" he wrote; yet people snubbed him in horse-cars, ministers maligned him in pulpit and press, and the Harvard faculty gave him scant recognition. The change of scene from Toledo to Cambridge in 1873, nevertheless, brought a new measure of happiness to him and his family. At first they lived on Shepard Street (No. 56), only fifteen minutes from Harvard Square. In 1876 they took a place out on Lakeview Avenue (No. 13), where there were the compensations of open country and boating on Fresh Pond, though not until 1880 did his negligent landlord build "a decent fence round the house, high enough to keep out the horses, cows, etc." Both houses were comfortable, allowing adequate space for the frequent guests and a servant girl. Frank's study became his private castle, and for the first time in his life all of his books and files were in one place. Two ivy plants inspired his efforts: one obtained from Theodore Parker's widow, who took it from her husband's study; the other from the plant that grew on Parker's grave in Florence.

Associations that sprang from Free Religious interests did provide intellectual diversion, and the proximity of "friends of liberalism" made it possible to establish quorums for all the boards and committees to which he belonged. The "Radical Club," which had offered such stimulation to the young minister of the late 1860s, continued to meet at the Chestnut Street home of John T. Sargent even after the venerable liberal died in 1877. The First Liberal League, of which Abbot was an officer, languished in the mid-1870s, but it generally held to a monthly schedule of meetings at which the usual topics of religion and morality were discussed. Frequently Abbot spoke at these meetings, and on other occasions at the Second League or Sunday morning services at Paine Hall.

His preaching at Unitarian churches was infrequent, consisting mostly of occasional "sermons" to Theodore Parker's old Twenty-Eighth Congregational Society. On request he would now and then fill the pulpits of some radical Unitarian friends. As usual he offered no prayers, preached a "thoroughly radical" sermon, and closed with a "free religious benediction." He attended Sunday services rarely, and then most often to hear some friend. Funerals provided his main excuse for entering Christian churches, and his remarks on the sermons were almost invariably critical. Sundays were more often devoted to outings with his children.

For Abbot, personally, the meetings with Unitarian clergy were sad, for he lamented the obstacles that his views placed between him and these fine men; but he could console himself that his work of the preceding thirteen years had had its visible effects.

Nothing could exceed the universal friendliness and even affection-
ateness of my reception by the Unitarian ministers, young and old.
I never felt before how deep an impression my thirteen years of
thought and protest have made. The change since Syracuse is wonderful. Only timidity keeps these men from openly siding with me;
for which I have only deep compassion—no blame. . . . I see how om-
nipotent is one man's isolated position, if it be the truth.
This is the dearest and most congenial fellowship in the world: I never
left it but for conscience's sake, with inextinguishable regret ever since
that I *must;* and it moves me almost to tears to see that they secretly
feel this *must,* and love me still.[4]

But others were not so willing to yield to such influences. Even old
C. A. Bartol criticized Unitarian invitations to Abbot, observing that
if liberalism were coming to this, there was need of orthodoxy. Abbot
was hardly a neutral party to such a dispute, and he was no doubt
pleased to print the strictures and rejoinders that seemed to justify his
authoritarian interpretation of Unitarianism.[5]

With the Cambridge academic community Abbot did not establish any real relationship until after his return from an ill-fated attempt to found a classical school in New York (1880-1881). Before that
his contacts were limited to the successful tutoring of a suspended student or two, and a series of brief, unpleasant conferences about ob-
taining a Ph.D. In 1877 William James had invited him to the meetings
of the "Philosophic Club," which was convening on the first occasion
at the home of Professor George H. Howison, but Abbot missed most
of these informal gatherings until after 1881. He did address the "Debating Club" of the Divinity School ("with the permission of the faculty") in February 1879, and in the next year he was asked to be one
of four speakers in a Harvard Philosophy Club lecture series, the other
three men being Professors William James, Charles C. Everett, and
George Herbert Palmer. On 1 March he gave his address on "Philosophy, the Guide of Life" to a large audience in Boylston Hall. In the
university community Abbot did not inspire a wide discipleship. He
had two "radical" followers in the Divinity School class of 1879, but
these men drifted away.

In Boston (as had been the case in Toledo, Dover, and elsewhere)
Abbot was plagued by financial difficulties. On one occasion (during

---

[4]Diary, 23 October 1879.

[5]See, in particular, the fracas over Abbot's invitation to address the Unitarian Ministers' Institute at Providence RI, as recorded in the *Index,* 30 October; 4, 11, 18 December 1879.

the winter and spring of 1878-1879) he took on a private pupil who had been separated from Harvard for bad grades. After spending two hours a day, five days a week for more than two months, he was able to get his charge back in school without conditions and uphold his reputation as a savior of even the most impossible pupils. During this period of tutoring he was able to say for the first time since 1868 that he was earning enough to meet the expenses of living. Nonetheless, he was unable to obtain another pupil on similar terms despite considerable advertising.

The main drain on his finances was the failing health of his wife. Katie had been troubled by various difficulties ever since the birth of their daughter in 1872. For a decade she had also been victim of a chronic complaint that she described as "pressure on the brain," and which gave rise to long and excruciating headaches. She began to fail the first winter in Cambridge, and already in 1875 she was dragging on his finances. In the spring of 1875 she "broke down completely" when their servant girl was found to have strangled her illegitimate baby in an upper bedroom of the house. In 1878 her condition became more acute and in October she began a long hospitalization at the women's and children's hospital in Roxbury.[6]

Frank, as well, was critically in need of rest and relaxation. His "old complaint," as he called the problem (prolapsus ani), continued to bother him, but the agony of hemorrhoids was not his only difficulty. Terrible headaches, which sometimes lasted for days, leaving him distracted and sleepless, rendered an increasingly large number of days unfit for constructive labors. Recurrent insomnia, only partly ameliorated by doses of "Vitalized Phosphates," sapped his energy. Nosebleeds came for no apparent reason while he would be riding on the horse-cars to or from Boston. And on more than one occasion he fell unconscious in his home without warning or special exertion. In November 1878 he felt his "whole nervous system . . . unstrung [and] vaguely dread[ed] a collapse of some kind." "I have not the strength of a rat nowadays," he wrote just before their vacation.

The remarkable fact is that Abbot had not long since collapsed. His schedule while he still worked on the *Index* was one of unmitigated routine. "The *Index* tells nothing of the business drudgery I do," he declared in his diary. "Mondays, Tuesdays, and Fridays I go to the Office, read the letters, do the multifarious business of the Associa-

---

[6]Diary, 2 May 1878. The following discussion of the health problems of the Abbot household is drawn from various references in Abbot's diary.

tion, etc. The rest of the week I devote to editorial work of all sorts in my study." Such a schedule, of course, might sound almost idyllic even to one acquainted with the Cambridge-Boston horse-cars; but there is much that this simple résumé does not tell. In the first place, the assiduity with which Abbot prosecuted his "editorial work" is unbelievable: it can only be guessed by one who has read the thousands of letters that he wrote to correspondents of the *Index* as well as an ever-widening circle of personal and business friends, or seen the record of countless meetings attended—often two or three a day—or gone through the weekly issues of the *Index* for which he wrote, arranged, and proofread so meticulously.

Over and above all this came the obligation that he felt in so solemn a way to make his own philosophic contribution. With him writing never came easily. There was never an approximate quotation of authors or evasive generalizing about factual matters. Whatever may be said for the originality of his thought, it can never be said that it was hastily conceived. It was hammered out, criticized, and rewritten time and again. There are few people who have labored so hard to say literally and explicitly what they meant, or done so under the frown of so many kinds of adversity.

A price would ultimately have to be paid for such exertions, and Abbot's closest friends were constantly urging him to relax his efforts, to relinquish some of his interests and, when possible, to enjoy a long, well-earned rest. In 1874 W. C. Gannett and Potter agreed to edit the *Index* for a month, but this was not repeated until 1877 when Sidney H. Morse, one-time editor of the *Radical,* took over for a month. A. W. Stevens, another friend, performed the service in the year following. Yet these temporary releases did little to reduce Abbot's cares and they required increased labors before and after vacations. His first and only real opportunity for rest and recovery came in July 1879 when he and Katie boarded a ship for the Azores. These two quiet months in the hotel at Horta, on the island of Fayal, became an idyllic memory. Here for the first time since his boyhood he had sustained leisure, and each day was profoundly enjoyed: the long hours in the hammock reading philosophy; trips into the country, he donkey-back, Katie in a hammock; the quiet talks as they sat by the sea-wall looking out over waters that generations of Larcoms and Ellingwoods had sailed.

On 14 September they were home again, and Abbot "plunged into a maelstrom of work, excitement, and anxiety." David H. Clark had done "extremely well" with the *Index,* but it soon became apparent that it would take more than improved health to rescue the situation. Frank's spirit was beyond resuscitation. For nine more months he fought the *Index*'s battles, then, as we have noted, committed it to other hands, and in doing so largely disassociated himself from the world of "liberal movements."

When Abbot left the world of "liberal movements," he turned down a path trod by innumerable kinsmen and became a teacher, founding a classical school in New York. It was to be a special type of school with not more than a dozen pupils, designed to provide essentially individual instruction so his tuition fees were correspondingly high. He went to New York in September and spent a year of hard work there (1880-1881), but the project failed. The drudgery broke his health, absence from his family crushed his spirit, and his reputation as an "infidel" ruined the prospect for students. After a year he fled his hot little bedbug-ridden room and returned to Cambridge, deciding to practice his pedagogy on a more limited scale from his home.

To help obtain students and to provide a motive for his philosophical work, he had obtained in 1879 the Harvard Academic Council's approval of his plans for a Ph.D., and the following May handed in his thesis, feeling that he had at least "put on paper the gist of the greatest philosophical system since the *Critique of Pure Reason* was published in 1781."[7]

But Francis Bowen, the conservative Unitarian professor of philosophy, had a less sanguine estimate of the writing and returned it with the remark that it was "so incomplete and imperfectly reasoned out that it is impossible to form any judgment of the merits." "That is the intellectual measure of that Committee," Abbot decided, attributing "the verdict" to other reasons that remain untold.[8]

Abbot immediately proceeded to enlarge the scope of his dissertation, this time deciding to synthesize his old *North American Review* articles, a rewritten form of his first thesis, and his lecture on Darwin's theory of conscience. He also resolved that if the committee rejected it, he would appeal to the Academic Council, requesting

> a new and competent committee, composed at least half of men thoroughly conversant with physical science and in full sympathy with the scientific method, and say plainly I had had no fair hearing from the committee of theologians. If I must have an issue, it shall be with H.U. [Harvard University] and not a sub-committee.[9]

---

[7]Ibid., 1-2 May 1880. See also 18 September 1879.

[8]Bowen to FEA, 29 May 1880; Diary, 1 June 1880.

[9]Diary, 21 April 1881.

This time he fared better. Both the thesis and his performance before the examination committee were satisfactory. On 29 June 1881 he received his diploma in Sanders Theater from President Eliot, "who smiled cordially as he gave it to me."

"Dr. Abbot" could now advertise a "Home for Boys" in the papers and promise "the best care in all respects" to pupils who would be boarded and trained for college. He had had to supplement his income at first, but by 1883 he had established himself as a master who got results; he then had little trouble enrolling three or four students. Reflecting on his $5,000 per year salary, he noted that he might have been moderately rich if he had turned to teaching in 1868, but in the present he always regarded the routine as a "treadmill." Six or eight hours of recitations and two or three of preparation shunted philosophical labors into the background.

He longed for a situation that would free him from teaching duties, but none came. In 1881 there had been a glimmer of hope for appointment to a chair of ethics and philosophy at Johns Hopkins, but his application was ignored. Rowland G. Hazard, a millionaire Free Religionist, advanced his cause, but President Daniel Coit Gilman feared what Abbot's reputation would do to the school's financial support. In 1886 President Eliot offered him a half-time position as an assistant librarian at Harvard, but Abbot could not bear to sacrifice a full summer vacation. Later in the year he proposed that Harvard accept him as the first occupant of a chair in philosophy that friends were willing to endow, but Eliot replied that Abbot's name would be too damaging to the university's reputation.

Only in 1889-1890 did the circumstances change. A series of gifts and legacies finally gave him that financial independence he had always lacked. Finally the way to a life of thought seemed clear.

CHAPTER TEN

SCIENTIFIC THEISM

AS WE PREVIOUSLY NOTED, in the great crisis of his junior year in college Abbot abandoned the postadolescent skepticism that he had learned at the feet of John Randall and returned to the faith of his mother and her spiritual hero, Ephraim Peabody. For five years he remained a prayerful apostle of evangelical Unitarianism, holding out firmly against Theodore Parker and all of his advocates. In 1862 he proved his piety to his old college roommate, a loyal Episcopalian: "If you can only see a love to God, a devotion to Christ and a deep yearning for man, in my preaching, I know you will feel I am still one in the Spirit with you . . . let God name us both Christians. For the love of Christ shall make us one forevermore."[1]

During the year following, important changes were introduced. Darwin, von Humboldt, and the scientific method made their impress, and the miracles of the New Testament began to create problems. By 1863 his philosophical studies had set him on the road of "reverential radicalism." The Atonement lost its traditional meaning; he became convinced that the "world would now be better off [if the Jews had] refused to add their great crime to the sum of human iniquity."[2]

With regard to literary influence, O. B. Frothingham came to be of major importance, as Abbot revealed in an effusive letter of gratitude written to him shortly after settling in Dover.

> I have been re-reading your "Birth of the Spirit Christ"; and the glow it had kindled is the only, but perhaps the sufficient, warrant for addressing you without a personal acquaintance. I feel moved to express, however inadequately, the indebtedness of our times to your earnest, free and reverent thought. The mantle of the supernatural, with which the Christ has been enveloped by a superstitious gratitude, is destined to fall away forever; and though with a poet's love of beauty you pay deserved homage to the cunning workmanship of

---

[1]FEA to James Fay, 17 May 1862; see also, FEA to Chaney, 26 November 1859.

[2]FEA to Chaney, early in 1863, probably January (letter not dated).

the human artist, in the higher interest of truth, you gently remove it, that you may display the naked grandeur of God's own handiwork. The Spirit Christ attests itself, and all other attestation is an impertinence and irrelevancy.[3]

During the next four years he tried desperately to contain his philosophical development within the framework of his Christianity, utilizing every device in the language to accomplish it. He failed, though. His sermons record the progress of his rationalism and the evaporation of his faith. Articles, speeches, and deeds elaborate the transition in great detail, but the Syracuse conference of 1866 and the Dover troubles produced the definitive break. To Chaney, who disagreed so utterly with his every word, he poured out the reasons.

> There is a higher gospel than that of Jesus . . . we must leap into sympathy with God by the intensity of our own aspirations, and look back on the N.T. from that loftier Mount of Vision. We can never divine the secret of our own spirits by peering into the depths of Jesus's— we must divine the secret of his spirit by peering into the depths of our own. There do we find God, the deepest depth of all,—and in the light that streams from him, the life of Jesus grows marvellously in power and beauty.[4]

Two years later he "came out from Christianity" entirely, and his theological revolution was complete. Philosophy, not theology, became the quest for Abbot.

Philosophically Abbot's thought shows a consistent development. In his last year of college he showed, if anything, less confidence in reasoned philosophy than his mentors, but at Harvard Divinity School he revolted from this leadership, especially when it sponsored Sir William Hamilton and Henry L. Mansel. It was to these thinkers that Abbot later attributed "the great service of awakening my philosophical consciousness,—not, it is true, by the way of agreement, but by way of polarization to opposite opinion." While perfecting his scholarly critique of those who would put knowledge of God beyond reason, his scientific theism emerged in his sermons.[5]

The aspiration that was to inform his whole philosophic effort was that philosophy had failed to achieve a fixed point of departure and sure method of advance. Abbot, clearly enough, was interested in pe-

---

[3]FEA to Frothingham, 26 September 1864.

[4]FEA to Chaney, 15 November 1866.

[5]Christie, *Makers of Meadville*, 121 (source not given).

rennial philosophy and confident that a "new era" would issue from his work; but he knew perfectly well that he was at the same time completely at odds with the temper of his own time. It is instructive, therefore, to consider the milieu in which he carried on his philosophic enterprise and identify the factors that, temporarily at least, doomed his acceptance.

The intellectual situation of the late-nineteenth-century world was conditioned first of all by the background of Christian faith and apologetics. The major thinkers, however diverse, tended to be affirmatively Christian or silent on the issue. Their common assumptions justified a remark such as that made to Abbot by Edward C. Towne: "You have rejected Christian superstition, but you have no more rejected Christian Religion than you have rejected North America."[6]

The pervasive influence of German idealism was a second and closely correlated factor. Abbot had learned this fact during his protracted battle with Transcendentalism; and his countless meetings with the Hegel Club, led by W. T. Harris, reinforced the earlier lesson. He thought the club's study of the *Logic* a "tiresome thrashing of straw," but he knew at the same time that idealism was too "firmly intrenched in the philosophic consciousness" of the day to permit the acceptance of realism. He saw those influences at work not only in committed men like Harris, Everett, and Royce but in William James and John Fiske as well.

A third element was evolution. Abbot had crossed swords with Herbert Spencer directly after the Civil War, and all through the 1870s he had warred against materialists and agnostics of the Spencerian stamp, so he was intensely aware of their message and their strength. Through enthusiasts of the doctrine such as Fiske and Frederick May Holland, moreover, it bore directly upon his own thinking. By 1880, when Abbot turned again to serious philosophical writing, the greatest period of Spencer's popularity was over but the general acceptance of "evolutionism" made its passing more apparent than real. Nor can there be any doubt that the experimental basis granted to the act of evolution and the dignity this and countless other scientific achievements conferred on experimental methods generally were fundamental factors in overthrowing the reign of post-Kantian doctrines.

These same scientific motives conditioned the ways of thinking that evolved from the interaction of Chauncey Wright, James, Peirce, and the other "founders of pragmatism." But the "neutrality of sci-

---

[6]Towne to FEA, 5 September 1870.

ence" affirmed by Wright, the impulsive irrationalism of James, and the Schellingian views of Peirce hardened Abbot's conviction that in his age even the men who recognized the claims of science would not accept a realistic philosophy, or a philosophy in which the world *in itself* could be known. In any event, it was in the crosscurrents of idealism, Spencerian positivism, and pragmatism—and against a genteel Christian background—that Abbot carried on his philosophical labors.

In contrast to all of these currents Abbot set forth his own philosophical position, which he called "Critical Realism." Abbot's critical realism was a philosophical approach not unrelated to the doctrine later propounded under that name by Durant Drake, George Santayana, C. A. Strong, and others. He also considered himself, justifiably, to be championing the moderate realism that had preceded the great nominalistic digression of modern times. In this sense, his thought is related to modern neo-Thomist and neo-Scotist philosophy. In the brief résumé that follows, however, it is not purposed to consider the sources, validity, or influence of these ideas but only to indicate the main lines of the system to which Abbot painfully devoted his life. Such an exposition is best initiated by considering Abbot's interpretation of the history of Western philosophy, which he stated most succinctly in the introduction to his *Scientific Theism.*

The famous passage from the preface to the *Critique of Pure Reason,* in which Kant describes his Copernican revolution, is Abbot's point of departure.

> Let us, then [Kant said], make the experiment whether we may not be more successful in metaphysics if we assume that the objects must conform to our cognition. . . . If the intuition must conform to the nature of the objects, I do not see how we can know anything of them *a priori.* If, on the other hand, the object conforms to the nature of our faculty of intuition, I can then easily conceive the possibility of such an *a priori* knowledge.[7]

Abbot denied that it was Kant who accomplished this revolution, attributing it rather to the emergence of nominalism in the philosopher Roscellinus in the latter part of the eleventh century and William of Occam in the fourteenth. The essence of this victorious view he described as "the doctrine that universals . . . correspond to nothing really existent outside of the mind."

---

[7]*Scientific Theism* (Boston, 1885) 1-2.

Nominalism distinctly anticipated the Critical Philosophy in referring the source of all general conceptions (and thereby of all human
knowledge), not to the object alone or to the object and subject together, but to the subject alone; it distinctly anticipated the doctrine
that "things conform to cognition, not cognition to things." . . . Kant
did but bring to flower and fruitage the seed sown by Roscellinus and
his Critical Philosophy was only the logical evolution and outcome of
Mediaeval Nominalism.[8]

After such an analysis of Kant it only followed naturally that he
ranged the philosophies of Fichte, Schelling, and Hegel under the
same rubric. As for the British tradition, he designated "Locke's successors, Berkeley, Hume, Hartley, the Mills, Bain, Spencer, and others" as equally led astray. And the Scottish school as well had been so
"paralyzed" by nominalism that its protest against sensationalism in
the name of common sense "died on its tongue."[9]

In response to this dismal history of philosophy Abbot boldly set
forth his own views—predicated upon his axiom, "knowledge exists."
Modern philosophy erred in not using the same assumptions as modern science, or the assumption that there existed not only "individual
knowledge" but a "universal knowledge," which has been substanti-
ated by verification and certified by the unanimous consensus of the
competent. "Science does not present its truths as anybody's states of
consciousness," he argued, "but as cosmical facts, acknowledgment of
which is binding upon all sane minds."[10] Although usually left unar-
ticulated, the principles that science *did* use were, he said, those of
scientific realism, or "Relationalism," as he termed it. This working
point of view, he went on, could best be designated as a theory of
Universalia inter res. It was directly related to the "three-fold" solution of certain medieval schoolmen who agreed that universals exist
as (1) *Universalia ante rem,* in the mind of God; (2) *Universalia in re,*
as the essence of things; and (3) *Universalia post rem,* as concepts in
the mind, of which words are vocal symbols. Abbot went beyond this
formulation, however, and argued that universals inhered objec-
tively not in individuals as *individuals* (*in re*) but in individuals *as*

---

[8]Ibid., 3-4.

[9]Ibid., 5-10. Abbot's omission of Sir Francis Bacon here is significant. He
saw Bacon as the unwitting formulator of principles essential to the progress
of science and hence as a critic of nominalism despite an inadequate understanding of Aristotle.

[10]Ibid., 10-11.

groups (*inter res*), and accordingly that we can have true knowledge of these individuals as groups.

> [U]niversals, or genera and species, are *first,* objective relations of resemblance among objectively existing things; *secondly,* subjective concepts of these relations, determined in the mind by the relations themselves; and, *thirdly,* names representative both of the relations and the concepts, and applicable alike to both.[11]

According to Abbot, this objective reality *inter res* had to be the basis of any true and certain knowledge. Kant had undermined this foundation, however, by making "relation" simply one of the four forms of logical judgment. In Abbot's schema the relation of things existed with the things *themselves* and not in the mind.

As Abbot pursued this matter further he demonstrated that the so-called "problem of Knowledge" stemmed from nominalistic assumptions that did indeed make it difficult to see how individuals "know" anything. The great division of modern European thought into sensationalists and rationalists was therefore basically a mere subcategory of the problem. Abbot thought both schools "immured . . . in the dungeon of subjectivism" and had no interest in releasing either of them. He saw Descartes positing an "*individual thinking* being" and Locke an "*individual* feeling or *sensing* being," both models being incontrovertibly egoistic.[12]

In his Harvard lectures Abbot summed up the history of modern philosophy and indicated his own purposes in a single sentence.

> In the German theory of Universals lies the deep, secret, and generally unsuspected source of all modern *Agnosticism,* a result which was uncritically accepted, ready-made, by Spencer and Huxley from Hamilton and Mansel, borrowed by Hamilton and Mansel from Kant and post-Kantian Idealists, and originally developed by Kant out of Hume and other adherents of Scholastic Nominalism.[13]

The "German Theory," here castigated, denied that any real intelligible genera in nature are accessible to the human mind. In other words, Abbot blamed the Germans for continuing the great separation of the phenomenal and the noumenal, or the idea that "man can know nothing of the object as it is in itself," and hence lacked any cer-

---

[11]Ibid., 25.

[12]Ibid., 34-39.

[13]*The Way Out of Agnosticism* (Boston, 1890) 17.

tain knowledge of the world. What Abbot wanted to do was to verbalize "the silent method of science." This method, he said, taught that

> knowledge is a dynamic correlation of object and subject, has two ultimate origins, the cosmos and the mind; that these origins unite, inseparably yet distinguishably, in experience . . . ; that experience . . . is the one proximate origin of knowledge; that experience has both an objective and a subjective side, and that these two sides are mutually dependent and equally necessary; . . . that this extended conception of experience destroys the distinction of noumena and phenomena, as merely verbal and not real; that "things-in-themselves" are partly known and partly unknown; that, just so far as things are known in their relations, they are known both phenomenally and noumenally, and that the possibility of experimentally verifying at any time their discovered relations is the practical proof of a known noumenal cosmos, meeting every demand of scientific certitude and furnishing the true criterion and definition of objective knowledge.[14]

In propounding a wiser doctrine, Abbot called for a "Retreat upon Aristotle" as preparation for a subsequent "advance to Darwin." As an introduction to the Aristotelian treatment of universals Abbot entered upon an exceedingly detailed analysis of self-consciousness (that is, of our conceiving of the ego or I). His purpose was to destroy the idea of the "bifurcation of the universe" into the ego and the non-ego. Ego-knowledge depended on knowledge of other consciousnesses; the I and the We were thus interrelated; an I presupposed a We. "It is [thus] a bald self-contradiction to say, 'We doubt . . . an external world;' for the 'We' thus posited . . . is itself, to every I, a world partly internal and partly external, and explicitly affirms what the judgment denies."[15]

The source of this vexing antithesis of the ego and non-ego Abbot traced (with considerable aid from Edward Zeller, the famous neo-Kantian) to the "Aristotelian Paradox," which grew out of Aristotle's attempted compromise of the issue between Plato and Antisthenes that concerned the Socratic separation of experience and reason. Aristotle opposed the Platonic ontological dualism of idea and phenomena; but while admitting with Plato that the universal was the only knowable essence and that the truth of our concepts depended on the reality of their object, Aristotle *also* declared with Antisthenes that the individual is the only real substance.[16]

---

[14]Ibid., 23; *Scientific Theism*, 39-40.

[15]*The Syllogistic Philosophy, or Prolegomena to Science*, 2 vols. (Boston, 1906) 1:147.

[16]Ibid., 1:156, 166-68.

Aristotle's doctrine of form and matter was designed to overcome Plato's dualism: the universal inhered in things always; form was the essence and substance of things. But Aristotle never questioned the basic principles of the concept-philosophy and consequently there remained no way of truly knowing the accidents that together with the individual essence made up the individuality of things. It was this, according to Abbot's criticism, that prevented a scientific understanding of the "totality of accidents" that constituted an individual, or "specimen" within a "species." "In fact, the Aristotelian conception of species has no conceivable ground whatever of any plurality of specimens." Hence for Aristotle "the individual thing . . . is completely unknowable . . . [since] it can only be *perceived;* and perception is not scientific, that is, conceptual knowledge. . . . The Aristotelian dualism of perception and knowledge, therefore, is absolute and irremediable." "The individual thing in itself . . . eludes knowledge altogether. . . . As an object of perception, it cannot be known at all; as an object of knowledge, it has lost its individuality." "For precisely these reasons and as a matter of course, the Aristotelian psychology includes no clear doctrine of human individuality . . . or personal unit."[17]

Now on first appearance this seems to be a return to Aristotle only to damn him, but such is not the case. Abbot did, to be sure, trace all the ills of modern philosophy to the unsatisfactory situation in which Aristotle left the problem of the relationship of experience and reason, and to the way in which it left matters open for far worse, or nominalistic, interpretations. His accusation, insofar as it was one, was that Aristotle's philosophy could not be adjusted to the dynamic conception of the universe propounded by modern science. He criticized Aristotle in the light of evolutionary theory for his failure to extend his analysis further beyond Plato so as to justify rationally our scientific knowledge not only of unique kinds (species) but of unique individuals. There were no "accidents," declared Abbot.

The Darwinian revolution in science was an unconscious revolution in philosophy, a purely practical abandonment of the Aristotelian Paradox, with its abstract and immutable species, for the scientific theory of universals, with its concrete and mutable species. The passage from one to the other was effected by recognizing the truth which Aristotle failed to discover: namely, that *the individual difference is*

---

[17]Ibid., 1:159-64 (emphasis added).

essential to the whole individual, and the whole individual is essential to the whole species.[18]

"The cardinal defect of the Aristotelian Paradox [Abbot went on] . . . lies in its exclusion of the individual difference from the individual essence, and its consequent incompetence to distinguish between the essence of the specimen and the essence of the species."[19] Aristotle had said that perception is of the Such (that is, the species), but not of the This (that is, the individual specimen). Abbot disagreed: "Perception is always of the This, and never of the Such—always of the unit, and never of the universal; the unit must be *perceived,* and the universal must be *conceived,* while at the same time the unit cannot be perceived unless the universal is conceived. . . . This is only to say . . . that the two acts of perception and of conception . . . condition each other absolutely in every possible cognition."[20]

In answering the profound question as to why the origins of human knowledge must be limited to experience and reason, Abbot revealed the ontological basis of his epistemology and delineated what Kant had called the "common but unknown root" of the two modes of human activity.

> Since, therefore, existence is possible only as the "something" or unit-universal, *knowledge is possible only as perception of the unit and conception of the universal in one indivisible percept-concept of the unit-universal.* The ultimate necessity of the two-fold branching of the knowing-faculty, therefore, is ontological, not ultimately epistemological or psychological; it must be "rooted" in the nature of the object, no less than in the nature of the subject; the percept-concept is the only actual or possible form of knowledge, (1) *because* the unit-universal is the only actual form of existence, and (2) *because* the unit-universal must be known as it is, or not at all. In other words, the only possible modes, functions, or faculties of knowledge are, from the sheer necessity of the case, in the uncreated "nature of things," those two forms of activity of the one knowing-faculty which, on the side of the unit, we call sensibility or perception or experience, and, on the side of the universal, understanding or conception or reason.[21]

Abbot thus carried the motif of evolution into the very fundament of his system. Every individual thing was a double product composed

---

[18]Ibid., 1:175.

[19]Ibid., 1:183.

[20]Ibid., 1:177 (emphasis added).

[21]Ibid., 1:206-207.

of three distinguishable elements. Through its *generic* essence in the genus and its *specific* essence in the species it partook of what was beyond it. In this sense "heredity" was the origin of its common element or community. The totality of individual "accidents" made up its larger *reific* essence, and "adaptation" was the origin of this individuality. Conception was thus made necessary by "hereditary" essences and perception by the "adaptive" (reific) essence. Yet a thing was always *one* thing and the essences were inseparable.

It was by this route that Abbot arrived at his central argument, namely that the evolution of the universe and the growth of true knowledge were part of the same wonderful unity.

> Every "something," as product, comes into existence through evolution, as process, and this process is the identity in difference of heredity and adaptation; hence *cognition* of the "something" as product, equally comes into existence through evolution, as process, and this process is identity in difference of perception and conception. The process of evolution, by which the "something" comes into existence, and the process of learning, by which it comes into knowledge, are at bottom one and the same, because the former necessarily determines the latter, as the condition of its reality. That is, learning is the evolution of all our knowledge: through conception and words we *inherit* the universality of the "something" and through perception we *adapt ourselves to* its unity. These fundamental analyses or definitions of existence and knowledge may be condensed into the form of continued equations.[22]

Every syllogism was thus a highly complex percept-concept and every percept-concept a virtual syllogism mediating implicitly between the specimen and the genus by the species. He summarized this principle in his Harvard lectures.

> The individual is a known fact; society is no less a known fact; but each is known only through the other, and what makes either known is what makes both known at the same time. [Elsewhere he used the example of the family and the meaninglessness of the word "daughter" as an isolated term.] . . . Upon this great principle of the *reciprocal revelation of thing and kind* rests, on the one hand, the possibility of *induction,* or reasoning from the constitution of a universal kind to that of its individual things.[23]

---

[22]Ibid., 1:207-208.

[23]*Way Out of Agnosticism,* 41.

By extending this line of reasoning to the problem of the ego and the non-ego, Abbot made a rational transition from the I to the We. Kant's "common but unknown root" of experience and reason was therefore no psychologically discoverable source but the *nature of being* and, derivatively, the nature of thought and the nature of knowledge. Abbot thought himself to be at the opposite pole from "Graeco-German *a priorism*," which he felt to rest on two erroneous postulates, namely: (1) that it was possible to separate as well as distinguish experience and reason in the empirical-rational ego (*der mit vernunft begabte Sinnenmensch*); (2) that it was possible to criticize or investigate reason *minus* experience in the purely rational or "pure" ego. "Knowledge of the I is necessarily knowledge of the We; knowledge of the We is necessarily knowledge of the external world; if I know enough to know myself as a unit-universal, I know my knowledge of the external world, since knowledge of either is knowledge of both."[24]

It is not necessary to consider Abbot's critique of the attempted transitions from the I to the We in Kant, Fichte, and Hegel, though these were probably once the most controversial chapters in the book. Nor does space allow detailed presentation of the broader metaphysical and religious implications of the basic analysis. The crux of the system was that the universe is intelligible because it is an immanent relational constitution: being, thought, and knowledge were corollaries. In attempting to fathom whether this relational constitution was an infinite machine, organism, or person, he argued that the only theory that did justice to the demands of thought or morality and the evidences of teleology was the conception of it as organism and not as machine. Therefore, since only infinite intelligence could create an infinite, intelligible, relational constitution he went on to personify the infinite organism. The "God of Science" therefore was pantheistically conceived. Yet Abbot insisted that God was a person.[25] He declared as well that "every deeply religious philosophy must hold fast, at the same time [to] the two great principles of the Transcendence and the Immanence of God; and that [the principle] of his Immanence, thought down to its foundation, is Monism. If God is not conceived as transcendent, he is confounded with matter. . . . But, if he is not conceived as immanent, he is banished from his own universe as a Creator *ex nihilo* and mere Infinite Mechanic."[26]

[24]*Syllogistic Philosophy,* 1:213-14.

[25]*Way Out of Agnosticism,* 47-75.

[26]*Scientific Theism,* 213.

Abbot's ethical theory was based on his ontological relationism. He discerned in the total world process a twofold development: *evolution* and *involution;* the former being immanent, indwelling, selfish, and self-preserving—the familiar stock-in-trade of social Darwinism; the latter, outgoing, altruistic, and self-devoting. This "Exient End" was characterized as an organism's devotion of self to "the preservation and evolution of the *higher self or species,* to which the individual Organism is related as the organ or organic cell is related to the Organism itself."[27] Since, for Abbot, a unit or individual was always related in an ascending scale of species and genera to the Absolute, the Exient End on one level was absorbed by the Immanent End on the next level, and so on. This became the basis for a thoroughly organismic interpretation of society.

He proceeded, therefore, to the proposition that "all right[s] and all duties,—all the facts of conscience with which Ethics deal,—are social in their nature." They simply would not exist were man not in society. Morals, or social duties, are "objective and universal relations among all moral beings," and ethics deals with these relations. "It follows that Ethics are one of the sciences, as truly as astronomy or geology."

> In other words, the Moral Obligation which constitutes the groundwork of all society, that is, the coexistence of moral beings in social relations, and which is the subject-matter of Ethics as one of the natural sciences, is simply a part of the ultimate Nature of Things. . . .
> It would be absurd to suppose a square whose two triangles should not be equal; and it would be just as absurd to suppose two moral beings in social relations without being under mutual moral obligation. There is, therefore, no rational escape from the conclusion that "Moral Obligation is an Objective Reality, and Scientific Ethics are Grounded on the Nature of Things."[28]

At this point he admitted the word *intuition* into his philosophy—but considering the way the term had been used by the proponents of Scottish commonsense philosophy in the antebellum period, it was placed under heavy guard. *Moral Intuition* was the "immediate perception" by an individual of the objective moral obligation: it was the reflection of the obligation in consciousness. Here there was room for

---

[27]*Way Out of Agnosticism,* 69-70 (emphasis added).

[28]*Darwin's Theory of Conscience: Its Relation to Scientific Ethics* (Boston, 1874) 13-15. This Horticultural Hall lecture is Abbot's most concise ethical statement.

error, but "increasing knowledge" gradually removed it, a fact that explained to Abbot "why the moral judgments of mankind became more and more alike in proportion as they become civilized." *Moral Sentiment* was merely the feeling in the person that he or she *ought* to act according to his intuition of moral obligation. *Moral Power* was the ability (varying among individuals) to act in accordance with this feeling. Such were the three elements of conscience.[29]

As Abbot brought this theory to more concrete application, he pointed out that individual "rights" and social "duties" were merely two aspects of the same principles. Each individual had a right to existence, freedom, and development; social duties involved the protection of life, the respecting of freedom, and the promotion of development. The "motives" of scientific ethics thus became reverence for the nature of things (truth), reverence for human nature (virtue), and reverence for society (love). Correct moral judgments, therefore, were not—as associationists and utilitarians urged—responses conditioned to eliminate pain or calculations to increase happiness, nor were they—as sentimentalists urged—a priori pronouncements of the conscience or of God in man. Ethics, he said, must go deeper and determine scientifically through the consensus of the competent the rights and duties of human beings as they obtained in nature. "Competence" required awe and understanding of man, God, and the universe, but Abbot never defined the credentials. "Competency is its own attestation."[30]

---

[29]Ibid., 20-22.

[30]This final statement is from an address he gave to the Harvard Divinity School. Printed in *Index,* 6 March 1879.

CHAPTER ELEVEN

THE FINAL YEARS

PHILOSOPHY MAY HAVE BEEN Abbot's primary devotion during his last two decades, but his life was not a philosopher's life. His final years did not see any miraculous transformation on a personal level. Old age and a final modicum of economic security brought neither contentment nor peace to him. Rather, continuing personal sorrows and professional frustrations marred even these "golden years."

His philosophizing brought him little peace. Indeed, although he viewed his ideas to be a form of good news to the divided world of modern philosophy, they involved him in what was perhaps the last major dispute of his career—a dispute that would be a major public concern within the intellectual circles of Boston in the 1890s.

In 1887 Josiah Royce, the great Harvard proponent of philosophical idealism, decided that an ocean voyage to Australia would help in the recuperation of his overstressed body and mind. During the semester that Royce was to be away, Abbot was chosen as the substitute lecturer for Royce's Philosophy of Nature course. Abbot later reworked these lectures and in 1890 published them under the title, *The Way Out of Agnosticism,* which can be seen as the culmination of many of the central issues Frank had been wrestling with since his Meadville days. In it his fundamental principle was forthrightly enunciated: that the modern world suffered from its inability to find a true grounding for knowledge, and that only through Abbot's own scientific method could both philosophical solipsism and religious agnosticism be avoided. Furthermore, on a personal level, he was also convinced that with the publication of the volume the world would finally shower upon his thought the recognition that it deserved.

As both a dedicated philosophical idealist and as a faculty member not yet possessing a professorship, Royce had both professional and personal reasons to be less than enthusiastic about Abbot's alleged "solution" to the problem of modern philosophy—a solution that so easily dismissed all other schools of thought. Hence in the first issue of the *International Journal of Ethics* Royce reviewed Abbot's volume with a devastating thoroughness. He not only dismissed Abbot's "unique" solution, or the American theory of universals, as a not particularly subtle borrowing from Hegel, but also set forth this challenge.

> But Mr. Abbot's way out is not careful, is not novel, and when thus set forth to the people as new and bold and American, it is likely to do precisely as much harm to careful inquiry as it gets influence over immature or imperfectly trained minds. I venture, therefore, to speak plainly, by way of professional warning to the liberal-minded public concerning Dr. Abbot's philosophical pretensions. And my warning takes the form of saying that if people are to think in this confused way, unconsciously borrowing from a great speculator like Hegel and then depriving the borrowed conception of the peculiar subtlety of statement that made it useful in its place—and if we readers are for our part to accept such scholasticism as is found in Dr. Abbot's concluding sections as at all resembling philosophy—then it were far better for the world that no reflective thinking whatever should be done. If we can't improve on what God has already put into the mouths of babes and sucklings, let us at all events make some other use of our wisdom and prudence than in setting forth the "American theory" of what in large part has been hidden from us.[1]

As might have been expected, Abbot was psychologically shaken by Royce's attack, which seemed to go beyond the bounds of scholarly disagreement into personal libel. Furthermore it seemed from Abbot's perspective that subsequently Royce used his professorial prerogatives and his position as a founding editor of the *International Journal of Ethics* to prevent Frank from adequately responding to his charges. Lawsuits were threatened, and the issue was appealed by Abbot to the Harvard Corporation and Board of Overseers, who exonerated Royce. Yet in the autumn of 1891 the literary public could read debate about the merits of the case in the *Nation* —articles written by some of the great lights of the American philosophical community.[2]

---

[1]Josiah Royce, "Dr. Abbot's 'Way Out of Agnosticism,' " *International Journal of Ethics* 1 (October 1890): 12-13.

[2]For Royce's view of the controversy, see the letters reprinted and the commentary provided in John Clendenning, ed., *The Letters of Josiah Royce* (Chicago: University of Chicago Press, 1970) 29-31, 272-73, 280-86. Abbot's reaction can be found not only in his diaries and letters but also in two published tracts: *Professor Royce's Libel: A Public Appeal for Redress to the Corporation and Overseers of Harvard University* (Boston, 1891); and *Is Not Harvard Responsible for the Conduct of Her Professors, as Well as Her Students? . . .* (Boston, 1892). Concerning the debate that took place within the

Nor did Abbot's nonphilosophical endeavors provide him much peace or contentment. After leaving the *Index* he had little time or desire for outside activities, but he did turn his hand to a few organizations. His most ambitious effort was the Boston Liberal Union Club, which began with informal dinner meetings that Abbot, with irrepressible desire for organization, soon formalized. He drafted a constitution, sent out letters to possible honorary vice-presidents, and on 31 March 1883 was himself elected president. As usual its purpose was "to advance the highest intellectual, moral, social, and religious interests of the community, and (as a means to this end) the highest interests of the Liberal, Ethical, or Free Religious Movement." The second article of the constitution stated that the club was designed "to vindicate the good name of Liberalism or Free Religion, now painfully tarnished." The meetings were monthly, partly for entertainment, partly for consideration of the moral aspects of public policy. The roster of officers revealed it to be a continuation of Abbot's other associative efforts. Occasionally, as when William Graham Sumner addressed them on "The Ethical Aspects of the Protective System," the attendance was large, but for the first few years it hovered around fifty per meeting, declining thereafter. Abbot finally withdrew as an officer in 1887, disgruntled over its loss of vitality and at odds with others' desire to allow newspaper reporters to attend meetings.[3]

From the F.R.A. Abbot all but withdrew. His opening address to the May convention of 1890 was his first appearance before the association in a decade, but it indicated no return to active duty. He gave a lecture on scientific ethics at a revived Horticultural Hall series in 1891; spoke twice at the Silver Jubilee of the F.R.A. in 1892; attended the 1893 meeting that joined the World Parliament of Religions at Chicago; and then, except for a brief effort to stimulate local societies, let the organization go its listless way.[4] With Unitarianism there came no rapprochement either, though he missed the warmth of ministerial fellowship more than ever. He scored Christian Unitar-

---

pages of the *Nation*, see 53 (12 November 1891): 372 for the views of Charles Peirce; 53 (19 November 1891): 389-90 for those of William James; and 53 (26 November 1891): 408 for those of J. B. Warner. See also, Bruce Kuklick, *The Rise of American Philosophy* (New Haven: Yale University Press, 1977) 250n for an insightful observation concerning the fracas.

[3]Diary, 29 March; 4, 12 May; and 3 November 1883.

[4]Ibid., 28 May 1890; 12 April 1891; 27 May 1892; 11-27 September 1893.

ianism in January 1885, in a letter to the *Christian Register* on the "Royalty of Jesus," beginning another debate with James Freeman Clarke that ran for several issues. Four years later radicals in the conference were successful in having him asked to address the national convention, but when the preamble question came up again in 1894, he was disappointed that Unitarianism acceded unanimously to follow "the religion of Jesus." "There is not a single genuine radical left in the Conference; . . . not a man voted for conscience at Saratoga." Abbot was alone and unaffiliated when he died.[5]

Only in politics during his last two decades did he revert to his earlier spirit, and this was indeed a startling change. In the past not all his moral fervor had ever led him either in the *Index* or elsewhere to show much interest in political or social problems. The abolition mystique had kept him alive to issues such as Reconstruction and the freed blacks; he favored women's rights; and in his last years he altered his earlier views to show a slight interest in temperance. He had been a mainline Republican from the beginning, favoring the impeachment of Johnson and backing Grant to the last; but by 1884 and the scandal-stained campaign of James G. Blaine, he had had enough. At the First Ward caucus during that campaign he precipitated the issue of moral opposition to Blaine. The caucus's ejection of Abbot signified the virtual exclusion of all but straight-ticket men from the party. He even carried his protest into the press and rejoiced in the election of Grover Cleveland. He never seems to have voted Republican again; and if he ever vacillated, the imperialism issue settled things once and for all, stimulating him to the final organizational efforts of his life. In July 1903, despite "sciatic tortures," he made his last public appearance via an address on "Emerson the Anti-Imperialist," almost collapsing before he finished.[6]

His political thought was never much elaborated, being for the most part conditioned by a limited type of "moral" consideration: a deviation from "sound" currency was robbery; Blaine was evil; the "sordid politics" of Harrison were a "disgrace"; Oliver Ames (the Republican candidate for governor in 1886) was a "money-bag nincompoop." Aside from "Southern issues," his most serious political thinking was provoked by his old classmate, Albert Stickney, whose extremely

---

[5]Ibid., 26 September 1894.

[6]Ibid., 26 August 1884; *Boston Evening Transcript*, 27 and 28 August 1884; Diary, 21 July 1903.

conservative, antiparty solution of democracy's problems Abbot regarded as classical for its penetration and thoughtfulness.

Abbot's life continued to be marked by personal sadness and loss. When poverty was not requiring him to spend the best hours of every day drilling students, the death of his mother and other loved ones clouded his mind and turned his quiet hours into orgies of grief. Perhaps even the countless hours devoted to genealogical researches, to the organization of societies for honoring the memory of the New England fathers, and countless committee meetings related to these peripheral organizations were merely other efforts to deprive the grave of its sting; but his philosophy suffered.

Furthermore, a severe melancholy began to overtake him after his wife's death in 1893. Her grave became not a shrine but a destination hoped for; life became an intolerable burden, a ritual of grief and commemoration.

In many ways the year 1903 seems to have been planned from the start. His brother Edward had died in 1863; his father had died in 1873; his mother in 1883, and Katie in 1893. "I must finish my book by October first without fail," he decided in February and by dint of constant self-denial he accomplished his purpose on 29 September: "A life-task done . . . At a quarter past twelve, midnight, I finish the last page. . . . I shall never reap a harvest from this seed—may it feed a world famine-struck for truth! . . . I have fought the good fight. *Nunc Dimittis*." Two weeks later the preface of *The Syllogistic Philosophy* was finished, and on a grey and rainy 18 October, Katie's birthday, he brought flowers to the grave in Beverly. In his diary he made his final apology.

> My life has not been a failure. Full of faults as it is, I have yet made it one long, faithful, and proud obedience to the *Logic of my Ideal* — unyielding, uncompromising, unvarying compliance with the logic of duty in every trial and temptation. This made me, still young, sacrifice my profession and all my hopes of University appointment— made me a slave to pinching poverty and social neglect. In this my gentle wife was my heroic helper and approver—God has no reward too great for her pure devotion to her husband's *best*. Now I die with my great life-task achieved. The world has shut me out of all high service save that [which] it could not prevent. I have won the fight, God be praised! If men know what truth is, or how to treasure it, my book will live for thousands of years. Imperfect as it is, it ought to be a wise guide to mankind for all time to come. Let God see to its fate.[7]

---

[7]Diary, 21 October; 28 February; 29 September 1903.

For the tenth anniversary of his wife's death (23 October), that day of inconsolable grief in 1893, the diary bears but a single word: "Heimkehr!" (return home).

The newspapers gave garbled stories of the event, and a New Bedford paper hinted that he had been mentally unbalanced. Still, the facts are clear enough. He consummated a plan that he had had in mind for many years and clearly laid out for at least a year. On 22 October he took a bouquet of carnations to the graves at Beverly, indicating that he would not be home for dinner. On the following morning, the anniversary of his wife's death, his failure to return led to a search; but nobody really doubted that he would be found at the cemetery. There he was, the flowers strewn about. He had taken poison during the night—his son Stanley saying after midnight on a priori grounds, the coroner saying before. With what acts and rites the deed was done none will know. A small and simple funeral, with no music and few guests outside of the immediate relations, followed on 26 October, with George Chaney officiating. He was cremated and, in accordance with the instructions of his will, laid beside Katie with a marker matching hers at his feet. Peace he had at last.

Perhaps there would have been no more fitting way for Abbot to have died. From his perspective, he died just as he had lived—unappreciated, but ultimately dedicated to the cause of truth. In his suicide note he proclaimed, "I do not fall out of this world by accident as a lunatic. . . . The great work on philosophy I was born to write is at last written . . . I bequeath it to my fellow men with the hope that it may help them to know God better, and make this world more noble, pure and just." Yet from any objective analysis Abbot's life cannot be taken on his self-declared terms, but rather must be reckoned a failure. Far from making the modern world more noble, pure, and just, Abbot and his great work made little positive impact on his era.

Part of the reason for this failure stems from Abbot's personality. In the name of purity and truth he continually alienated himself from potential support. A psychobiographer could find much grist in Abbot's unique gift of being able to derail or ruin almost every organization or cause to which he belonged. Much of the sense of frustration and spoiled potential that emanates from both his personal and public history must be attributed to his own doing.

On another level, however, Abbot failed in constructively instructing his generation because he developed and then, to the best of his ability, lived according to a system of thought that ran counter to all the prevailing speculative winds of doctrine in the United States. In the America of the late nineteenth century, one could not expect an enthusiastic audience for a point of view directed in the most belligerent fashion against the era's four most important trends in thought: evangelical Christianity, Spencerianism, idealism, and the emerging pragmatism. Under one or the other of these standards most American philosophers and theologians (amateur and professional) were ranged, and Abbot damned them all even though, as we have seen, he was influenced by them all. The intellectual life of Francis Ellingwood Abbot is as much the story of the perimeters of acceptable opinion during the last third of the nineteenth century as it is the story of one nonconformist. Indeed, this setting forth of the bounds of "acceptable" opinion was not simply an intellectual phenomenon, but an institutional one as well. Time and again Abbot found himself barred from an academic sinecure because of the unorthodoxy of his views. Bruce Kuklick has argued that the "professionalization" of American philosophy during the last decades of the nineteenth century served also to narrow the discipline. "It is a measure of what happened to speculation in the United States," notes Kuklick, "that the religious orthodoxy that contributed to Emerson's fame helped bar Abbot from institutional employment, so that posterity would forget him despite his intellectual strength."[8]

Personality problems on one side and sociological factors on the other are just two of the reasons that Abbot and his generation never really communicated with each other. They shared a set of common questions—the problem of revealed religion, the issue of science and religion, the philosophical concern with the avoidance of subjectivism, and the tensions between religion and the Republic and liberty and license—yet they came up with fundamentally different answers.

_____

[8]Kuklick, *The Rise of American Philosophy*, 102-103.

BIBLIOGRAPHY

It has been a major problem to keep this bibliography within reasonable bounds; and since we fail to see in it what Abbot would call an "immanent relational constitution," it has been as difficult to categorize the types of works omitted as those included. Except to express some special indebtedness, we have listed neither the great works of Western philosophy and theology nor standard secondary works such as Harnack's *History of Dogma,* Hoffding's *History of Modern Philosophy,* and the *Dictionary of American Biography.* At the other end of the scale, we have also omitted countless sermons, polemical pamphlets, and memoirs, as well as uncited, peripheral secondary treatments. The list of writings by Abbot is largely complete. Since we have excluded from this book any critical consideration of the sources, quality, and influence of Abbot's strictly philosophical endeavors, however, we have listed very few writings of other persons pertaining to these matters. For a more complete bibliography of earlier Unitarianism the reader should consult the bibliography found in *An American Reformation: A Documentary History of Unitarian Christianity,* ed. Sydney E. Ahlstrom and Jonathan S. Carey (Middleton CT: Wesleyan University Press, 1985).

I. THE ABBOT PAPERS

The basic source for the study of Abbot's life and work is the collection of personal papers that he assembled during his lifetime. He saved almost everything, while his son, Dr. Edward Stanley Abbot, and his daughter, Mrs. Ralph G. Wells, culled out only the more clearly irrelevant materials before presenting the collection to Harvard University. They abided as well by his expressed conviction that not even the most private papers should be withheld from a biographer.

From the beginning these materials were carefully filed and labeled; and in later years, while rereading them, Abbot made many explanatory remarks and cross-references. Though it would be impractical to list all the types of material included, there are five major classifications of documents. The first is Abbot's diaries, including those kept intermittently in childhood and Latin School, in college, in 1869, and continuously from 1877 until his death, as well as philosophical notebooks and commonplace books. The second is the prose and poetic writings—from childhood "scribblings" to his final lecture, including many never published. The third is the correspondence, amatory, casual, official, and philosophical, with all manner of relatives, friends, associates, and antagonists; this includes copies or originals of much from his own pen. The fourth is official and semiofficial records and correspondence of various organizations with which he was involved. Finally there is an extensive collection of pamphlets, programs, announcements, souvenirs, and clippings pertaining to his own life and related organizations.

Since Abbot's writings are so dispersed throughout little-remembered journals, they are listed here in detail in order to show the breadth of his interests. Two other sources of Abbot's writings should also be mentioned. Many of his best sermons were never published and can only be found in the Abbot Papers. Likewise issues of the *Index* contain a great quantity of Abbot's literary output. Most of the Horticultural Hall lectures and F.R.A. Convention addresses listed below were often reprinted there, but in addition its pages are a treasure chest of Abbot's ephemeral opinions.

II. BOOKS

Abbot, Francis E., ed. *Arethusa Hall; A Memorial.* Cambridge, 1892.

_____, ed. *An Early Scene Revisited* [poems of John Randall]. Cambridge, 1894.

_____, ed. *The Fairies' Festival* [poems of John Randall]. Boston, 1894.

_____. *In Foro Conscientiae.* Cambridge, 1894.

_____. *The Inside History of the Index Association.* Toledo, 1873.

_____, ed. *Poems of Nature and Life* [poems of John Randall]. Boston, 1899.

_____. *Scientific Theism.* Boston, 1885.

_____. *The Syllogistic Philosophy, or Prolegomena to Science.* Two vols. Boston: Little, Brown & Co., 1906.

_____. *The Way Out of Agnosticism, or the Philosophy of Free Religion.* Boston, 1890.

III. OCCASIONAL ESSAYS AND ARTICLES

Horticultural Hall Lectures

14 February 1869 "The Genius of Christianity and Free Religion." In *Freedom and Fellowship in Religion,* 222-64. Octavius B. Frothingham, ed. Boston, 1875. Also in *American Philosophic Addresses,* 680-708. Joseph L. Blau, ed. New York: Columbia University Press, 1946.

27 February 1870 *Jesus and Socrates in the History of Religion.* Boston, 1877.

 5 February 1871 "Intuitionalism versus Science, or the Civil War in Free Religion" (retitled: "The Intuitional and Scientific Schools of Free Religion").

11 February 1872 *The God of Science.* Boston, 1872.

 2 February 1873 *A Study of Religion: The Name and the Thing.* Boston, 1873.

22 February 1874 *Darwin's Theory of Conscience: Its Relation to Scientific Ethics.* Boston, 1874.

  21 March 1875 *Atomism in Science and Religion.* Boston, 1875.

20 February 1876 *The Public School Question as Viewed by the Liberal American Citizen.* (A debate with Bishop McQuaid of Rochester, New York) F.R.A. Tract No. 5. Boston, 1876.

  11 March 1877 *The Scientific Method in Religion.* Boston, 1880.

  12 April 1891 "The Scientific Basis of Ethics." (Unpublished MS in Abbot Papers.)

Free Religious Association Convention Addresses

1867 "Remarks." *Report of Addresses at a Meeting Held in Boston, May 30, 1867, to Consider the Conditions, Wants, and Prospects of Free Religion in America. Together with the Constitution of the Free Religious Association There Organized, 37-40.* Boston, 1867.

1868 "Remarks." *Proceedings of the Annual Meeting, 75-76.*

1869 "Remarks." Ibid., 35.

1870 "The Future of Religious Organization as Affected by the Spirit of the Age." Ibid., 43-51.

1873 "Remarks." Ibid., 86-94.

1874 "The Anti-Christian Attitude of Believers in Religious Freedom." Ibid., 41-49.

1875 "Construction and Destruction in Religion." Ibid., 47-58.

1879 "Remarks." Ibid., 58-64.

1880 "What Does Free Religion Offer as the Guide of Life?" *Proceedings* not published; see *Index,* 3 June 1880.

1890 "Moral Education and Personal Effort as Factors of Social Reform." *Proceedings* not published; see *New Ideal* 3 (July-August 1890): 288-98.

1893 "Scientific Method the Measure of Religious Progress." *Proceedings of the Annual Meeting, 36-50.*

Religious and Philosophical Essays

"The Advancement of Ethics." *Monist* 5 (1895): 192-222. Probably Abbot's best presentation of his conviction that "universalism" must be substituted for "individualism" and "objective justice" for "subjective."

Alexander von Humboldt: An Oration Delivered at the Centennial Celebration, September 14, 1869. Toledo, 1869. Published separately by the German-language *Weekly Express.*

"The American Trust Fund for the [Encouragement and] Publication of Liberal Thought" (MSS, May 1889, relating to the formation and purposes of said trust, including "Remarks" and formally proposed documents).

"The Book of Daniel." *Radical* 7 (1870): 28-42. First delivered as a Free Lecture in Dover, 30 January 1869. It well sums up Abbot's conclusions about the essential Messianism of Christianity.

"The Catholic Peril in America." *Fortnightly Review,* n.s. 19 (1876): 385-405. Reprinted in *Index,* 8 June and 15 June 1876, and as an *Index* tract.

"The Conditioned and the Unconditioned." *North American Review* 98 (1864): 402-48. [A review of Hamilton, Sir William, *Discussions of Philosophy and Literature, Education and University Reform.* New York, 1858; and Hamilton, Sir William, *Lectures on Metaphysics and Logic.* Volume two. Henry L. Mansel and John Veitch, eds. Boston, 1859-1860.]

"Creeds and Unitarianism." *Radical* 2 (1867): 571-73. A defense of his interpretation as "excluded" by the 1866 Preamble; it was refused publication by the *Christian Register.*

"The Dependence of Ethics." *New Ideal* 2 (1889): 26-27.

"Dr. Hazard's Place in the History of Philosophy." (MS, October 1888, written for a memorial volume that was never published. Abbot Papers.)

"The Ethics of Pulpit Instruction." *Christian Examiner* 83 (1868): 40-61. Delivered first as an address to the Ministerial Union, Arlington Street Church, 14 October 1867. A radical statement of the ministerial role.

"Free Religion, Not Agnosticism. A Card of Protest." *Index,* 30 December 1886.

"The Future of Philosophy at Harvard." *The Harvard Monthly* 5 (1887): 43-49.

"The Genius of Christianity and Free Religion." In *American Philosophic Addresses, 1700-1900,* 680-708. Joseph L. Blau, ed. New York: Columbia University Press, 1946.

The Influence of Philosophy upon Christianity. An address delivered 21 October 1879 to Unitarian Ministers' Institute in Providence RI. Boston, 1880.

"The Moral Creativeness of Man." *Journal of Speculative Philosophy* 18 (1884): 139-52.

"Moral Education and Personal Effort as Factors of Social Reform." *New Ideal* 3 (1890): 288-98.

"The National Unitarian Conference." *Christian Register* 45 (17 November 1866). An attack on creeds, and a rationale for regarding himself as excluded by the Syracuse convention.

"Organization." *Radical* 2 (1866): 219-25.

"Outlines of the Liberal Religious Situation." *Free Church Tracts* No. 1. Tacoma WA, 1895.

"The Philosophy of Free Religion." *New Ideal* 2 (1889). [These articles are the substance of Abbot's course at Harvard in 1888; they appear without major alteration as the *Way Out of Agnosticism,* above-listed.]

"The Philosophy of Space and Time." *North American Review* 98 (1864): 64-116. Not for twenty years, if ever, did Abbot display the philosophic incisiveness of this article and its companion article.

"Positivism in Theology." *Christian Examiner* 80 (1866): 234-67. [A review of Spencer, Herbert, *First Principles.* London, 1862.]

"A Radical's Theology." *Radical* 2 (1867): 585-97. In this early pronunciamento Abbot stated clearly his fundamental assumption, "deeper than any argument," that the universe is a harmonious unit. The universal scientific postulate was "Faith in the Universe."

[Review of Maudsley, Henry,] *The Physiology and Pathology of the Mind.* New York, 1867. *North American Review* 106 (1868): 277-86. A short "Critical Notice" making little constructive contribution, except insofar as it seeks to justify metaphysics.

[Review of Spencer, Herbert,] *Principles of Biology.* Volume Two. New York, 1866-1867. *North American Review* 108 (1868): 377-422. A major article that provoked Spencer, in reply, to add an appendix to vol. 1.

"Sectarianism." In *World Unity in Religion and Religious Organization.* Tacoma WA, 1900. This small volume contains Abbot's essays (3-21) followed by criticism and Abbot's replies (22-25).

"Scientific Philosophy: A Theory of Human Knowledge." *Mind, A Quarterly Journal of Psychology and Philosophy* 7 (1882): 461-95. This was part 3 of Abbot's thesis, later forming the introduction to *Scientific Theism,* above-listed.

"Theism and Christianity." *Christian Examiner* 79 (1865): 157-74. [A review of Hedge, Frederic H., *Reason in Religion.* Boston, 1865.]

"The Two Confederacies." *Christian Register,* 24 June 1865.

"What Makes a Church Free?" *Free Church Record* 4 (1896): 50-52.

Miscellaneous Essays

"Appeal to the Hon. Charles Francis Adams." Boston *Herald,* 23 May 1899. A lengthy remonstrance against the defection of a vice-president of the Anti-Imperialist League, in the form of an "open letter."

"Blaine and the Mugwumps." Cambridge *Tribune,* 12, 19, and 26 June 1884. Other public letters on the subject: Boston *Transcript,* 28 August 1884; Boston *Herald,* 2 September 1884.

"The Boston Tea Party." *New England Magazine* 8 (June 1893): 411-27. Abbot's oration to the Sons of the Revolution, at King's Chapel, 22 February 1893. He was pleased to point out that the colonial patriots had acted over a "moral trifle."

"Emerson the Anti-Imperialist." Abbot's final public lecture, 21 July 1903. MS, Abbot Papers.

"The Harvard Seal Controversy, a Letter and Sonnet." Boston *Herald,* 26 June 1887.

Is Not Harvard Responsible for the Conduct of Her Professors, as Well as of Her Students? A Public Remonstrance Addressed to the Board of Overseers of Harvard University. Boston, 1892.

Professor Royce's Libel: A Public Appeal for Redress to the Corporation and Overseers of Harvard University. Boston, 1891.

"Wagons and Stars." *Practical Ideals* 1 (1901). An appeal to quiet the imperialist temper.

IV. SECONDARY SOURCES

Ahlstrom, Sydney E. "Eliot, the Tutor and Fireman." *Harvard Alumni Bulletin* 51 (March 1949): 450-54.

Allen, Joseph Henry. *Our Liberal Movement in Theology.* Boston, 1882.

_____. *Sequel to "Our Liberal Movement."* Boston, 1897.

_____. *The Unitarian Movement since the Reformation.* American Church History Series. New York, 1894.

Auerbach, Berthold. *On the Heights.* F. E. Bunch, tr. Boston, 1868.

Bartol, Cyrus A. "Hedge's *Reason in Religion.*" *Christian Examiner* 79 (1865): 84-95.

Bellows, Henry W. "The National Conference of Unitarian and Other Christian Churches." *Christian Examiner* 85 (1868): 319-43.

Bennett, DeRobigne M. *Thirty Discussions, Bible Stories, Essays and Lectures.* New York, 1876.

Broun, Heywood and Margaret Leech. *Anthony Comstock: Roundsman of the Lord.* New York: Literary Guild, 1927.

Burggraaff, Winfield. *The Rise and Development of Liberal Theology in America.* New York: Board of Publication and Bible School Work of the Reformed Church in America, 1928.

Butterworth, George W. *Spiritualism and Religion.* London: Society for Promoting Christian Knowledge, 1944.

Calthrop, Samuel R., et al. *Charles DeBerard Mills.* Syracuse, 1900.

Carrav, Ludovic. *La Philosophie Religieuse en Engleterre.* Paris, 1888.

Chadwick, John W. *Old and New Unitarian Belief.* Boston, 1894.

Chapman, John Jay. *The Two Philosophers: A Quaint Comedy.* Boston, 1892.

Cheever, George B. *Right of the Bible in Our Public Schools.* New York, 1859.

Cheney, Ednah Dow. *Reminiscences*. Boston: Lee and Shepard, 1902.

Christie, Francis A. *Makers of Meadville Theological School, 1844-1894*. Boston: Beacon Press, 1927.

Clarke, James Freeman. "Letter . . . to Rev. Francis E. Abbot of Dover." *Christian Register,* 1 December 1866.

_____. *Orthodoxy: Its Truths and Errors.* Sixteenth ed. Boston, 1889.

_____. *Steps of Belief; or Rabonal Christianity Maintained against Atheism, Free Religion and Romanism.* Boston, 1870.

_____. *Ten Great Religions: An Essay in Comparative Theology.* Nineteenth ed. Boston, 1883.

Clemens, Cyril. *Petroleum Vesuvius Nasby.* Webster Grove MO: International Mark Twain Society, 1936.

Comstock, Anthony. *Frauds Exposed.* New York, 1880.

_____. *Traps for the Young.* New York, 1883.

Conway, Moncure. *Autobiography, Memories and Experiences.* Two vols. Boston and New York: Houghton, Mifflin and Co., 1904.

Cooke, George W. *Unitarianism in America: A History of Its Origin and Development.* Boston: American Unitarian Association, 1902.

Crooker, Joseph Henry. *The Unitarian Church: Its History and Characteristics.* Boston: American Unitarian Association, 1934.

Davis, Andrew J. *The Great Harmonia.* Five vols. Boston, 1855-1860.

Dirks, John Edward. *The Critical Theology of Theodore Parker.* New York: Columbia University Press, 1948.

Douglas, Ann C. *The Feminization of American Culture.* New York: Knopf, 1977.

Eliot, Charles W. *Harvard Memories.* Cambridge: Harvard University Press, 1923.

Eliot, Samuel A., ed. *Heralds of the Liberal Faith.* Four vols. Boston: American Unitarian Association, 1910-1952.

Emerton, Ephraim. *Unitarian Thought.* New York: Macmillan, 1910.

Foster, Frank H. *The Modern Movement in American Theology.* John H. Greene, ed. New York: Fleming H. Revell, 1939.

Frothingham, Octavius B. *Boston Unitarianism, 1820-1850: A Study of the Life and Work of Nathaniel Langdon Frothingham.* Boston, 1890.

_____. *Recollections and Impressions, 1822-1890.* New York, 1891.

_____. *Theodore Parker.* New York, 1886.

_____. *Transcendentalism in New England: A History.* New York, 1876.

Gannett, William C. *Ezra Stiles Gannett.* Boston, 1875.

Gross, Paul A. N. "John Gorham Palfrey." B.A. Honors Thesis, Harvard University Archives, 1951.

Hale, Edward Everett. "The National Conference of Unitarian Churches." *Christian Examiner* 78 (May 1865): 409-30.

Hardinge [Britten], Emma. *Modern American Spiritualism*. New York, 1870.

Hazard, Rowland G. *Causation and Freedom in Willing, Together with Man a First Cause, and Kindred Papers*. Boston, 1889.

_____. *Essay on the Philosophical Character of Channing*. Boston, 1845.

Hedge, Frederic H. "*The North American Review* on 'Space and Time.' " *Monthly Journal of the American Unitarian Association* 3 (1865): 134-40.

_____. *Reason in Religion*. Boston, 1865.

_____. *Recent Inquiries in Theology by Eminent English Churchmen: Being "Essays and Reviews."* Boston, 1860.

Herbold, Charles J. *The National Liberal League: What It Is and What It Is Not*. Cincinnati, 1880.

Heywood, Ezra H. *Cupid's Yokes: or the Binding Forces of Conjugal Life. An Essay to Consider Some Moral and Physiological Phases of Love and Marriage* . . . Princeton MA: n.p., n.d.

Higginson, Thomas Wentworth, ed. *Harvard Memorial Biographies*. Volume two. Cambridge, 1866.

Howe, Daniel W. *The Unitarian Conscience: Harvard Moral Philosophy, 1805-1861*. Cambridge: Harvard University Press, 1970.

Huntington, Arria S. *Memoir and Letters of Frederic Dan Huntington* . . . Boston and New York: Houghton, Mifflin & Co., 1906.

Huntington, Frederic Dan. *Christian Believing and Living*. Boston, 1860.

_____. "From Puritanism—Whither?" *Forum* 1 (1886): 314-26.

Hurlbut, Elisha P. *Essays on Human Rights and Their Political Guarantees*. Edinburgh, 1847.

_____. *A Secular View of Religion in the State; and the Bible in the Schools*. Albany, 1870.

Hutchison, William R. *The Modernist Impulse in American Protestantism*. Cambridge: Harvard University Press, 1976.

James, Henry. *Charles W. Eliot: President of Harvard University, 1869-1909*. Two vols. Boston and New York: Houghton, Mifflin & Co., 1930.

Johnson, Samuel. *The Worship of Jesus, in Its Past and Present Aspects*. Boston, 1868.

Johnston, Johanna. *Mrs. Satan: The Incredible Saga of Victoria C. Woodhull*. New York: Putnam, 1967.

Kring, Walter Donald. *Henry Whitney Bellows*. Boston: Skinner House, 1979.

Kuklick, Bruce. *The Rise of American Philosophy: Cambridge, Massachusetts, 1860-1930*. New Haven: Yale University Press, 1977.

Leopold, Richard W. *Robert Dale Owen*. Cambridge: Harvard University Press, 1940.

Lewis, Taylor. *Discourse on the True Idea of the State as a Religious Institution, Together with the Family and the Church Ordained of God.* Andover, 1843.

_____. *Plato contra Atheos: Plato against the Atheists.* New York, 1845.

Livermore, Abiel Abbot and Sewall Putnam. *History of the Town of Wilton.* Lowell MA, 1888.

Lothrop, Samuel K. *Reminiscences.* Boston, 1888.

Lyttle, Charles H., ed. *The Liberal Gospel.* Boston: Beacon Press, 1929.

McCabe, Joseph. *Spiritualism.* New York: Dodd, Mead & Co., 1920.

Marberry, M. M. *Vicky: A Biography of Victoria C. Woodhull.* New York: Funk and Wagnalls, 1967.

Miller, Perry. *Errand into the Wilderness.* Cambridge: Harvard University Press, 1956.

_____. *The Life of the Mind in America: From the Revolution to the Civil War.* New York: Harcourt, Brace and World, 1965.

_____. *The Transcendentalists: An Anthology.* Cambridge: Harvard University Press, 1950.

Mills, Charles DeBerard. *The Indian Saint: or Buddha and Buddhism.* Northampton MA, 1876.

_____. *Pebbles, Pearls, and Gems of the Orient.* Boston, 1882.

_____. *The Tree of Mythology.* Syracuse, 1889.

Moore, James L. *Introduction to the Writings of Andrew Jackson Davis.* Boston: Christopher Publishing House, 1930.

Morison, Samuel Eliot, ed. *The Development of Harvard University since the Inauguration of President Eliot, 1869-1929.* Cambridge: Harvard University Press, 1930.

_____. *Three Centuries at Harvard.* Cambridge: Harvard University Press, 1936.

Nenneman, Richard A. "Octavius Brooks Frothingham." B.A. Honors Thesis, Harvard University, 1951.

Owen, Robert Dale. *Footfalls on the Boundary of Another World.* Philadelphia, 1860.

Peabody, Andrew Preston. *Harvard Reminiscences.* Boston, 1888.

Peabody, Francis G. *Harvard in the Sixties: A Boy's Eye View.* Cambridge, 1935. [Reminiscences contributed to the Cambridge Historical Society at its meeting of 12 March 1935.]

Persons, Stow, ed. *Evolutionary Thought in America.* New Haven: Yale University Press, 1950.

_____. *Free Religion: An American Faith.* New Haven: Yale University Press, 1948.

Podmore, Frank. *Modern Spiritualism.* Two vols. London: Methuen, 1902.

Potter, William J. *The Free Religious Association: Its Twenty-Five Years and Their Meaning.* Boston, 1892.

——————. *Lectures and Sermons.* Boston, 1895.

——————. *Twenty-Five Sermons of Twenty-Five Years.* Boston, 1885.

Putnam, Samuel P. *Four Hundred Years of Free Thought.* New York, 1894.

Rand, Benjamin. "Philosophical Instruction in Harvard from 1836 to 1900." *Harvard Graduate's Magazine* 37 (1928-1929): 29-47, 188-200, 296-311.

Reynolds, Grindall, ed. *Unitarianism: Its Origins and History.* The Channing Hall Lectures. Boston, 1890.

Robinson, David. *The Unitarians and the Universalists.* Westport CT: Greenwood Press, 1985.

Royce, Josiah. "Dr. Abbot's 'Way Out of Agnosticism.' " *International Journal of Ethics* 1 (October 1890): 98-113.

Sachs, Emanie Louise. *The Terrible Siren* [Victoria C. Woodhull]. New York: Harper and Bros., 1928.

Sargent, Mrs. John T., ed. *Sketches and Reminiscences of the Radical Club of Chestnut Street.* Boston, 1880.

Schneider, Herbert W. *History of American Philosophy.* New York: Columbia University Press, 1946.

Slicer, Thomas R. *The Power and Promise of the Liberal Faith.* Boston, 1900.

Spencer, Herbert. *First Principles.* New York, 1883.

——————. *Principles of Biology.* Two vols. Edinburgh, 1864.

——————. *Spontaneous Generation, and the Hypothesis of Physiological Units.* New York, 1870.

Sprague, William B. *Annals of the American Pulpit* . . . Volume 8: *Unitarian Congregational.* New York, 1865.

Stange, Douglas C. *Patterns of Antislavery among American Unitarians, 1831-1860.* Rutherford NJ: Farleigh Dickinson University Press, 1977.

Suter, John Wallace. *The Life and Letters of William Reed Huntington.* New York and London: Century, 1925.

Throop, George R. "William Greenleaf Eliot." *Proceedings,* Unitarian Historical Society 4:1 (1933): 33-43.

Tilton, Theodore. *Victoria C. Woodhull: A Biographical Sketch.* New York, 1871.

Todd, E. W. "Philosophical Ideas at Harvard." *New England Quarterly* 2 (1929): 199-233.

Towne, Edward C. "Christianity and Pseudo-Christianity." *Christian Examiner* 82 (1867): 133-60.

——————. "The *Index* on Christianity Again." *Examiner* 1 (1871): 231-34.

——————. "The Radical Club of Boston; Its History and Its Headquarters." *Examiner* 1 (1871): 367-72.

——————. "Rev. Mr. Abbot's Position." *Examiner* 1 (1870): 127-46.

_____. *Unitarian Fellowship and Liberty: A Letter to [the] Rev. Henry W. Bellows, D.D.* Cambridge, 1866.

Underwood, Benjamin F. *Evolution in Its Relation to Evangelical Religion.* Boston, 1882.

_____. *The Influence of Christianity on Civilization.* New York, 1884.

Waller, Altina. *Reverend Beecher and Mrs. Tilton: Sex and Class in Victorian America.* Amherst: University of Massachusetts Press, 1982.

Ware, William. *American Unitarian Biography.* Two vols. Boston, 1851.

Warriner, Austin R. "The Crisis of Evangelical Unitarianism: A Study of the Problem of Faith and Freedom in Unitarian Thought: Being a Survey of the Origins of the Liberal Theology in New England and Its Conflict with Transcendentalism." B.A. Honors Thesis, Harvard University, 1951.

Wasson, David A. *Essays: Religious, Social, Political.* Boston, 1889.

_____ et al. *Freedom and Fellowship in Religion: A Collection of Essays and Addresses.* Boston, 1875.

_____. "Mr. Abbot's Religion." *Radical* 78 (1870): 408-21.

Wells, Ronald Vale. *Three Christian Transcendentalists: James Marsh, Caleb Sprague Henry, Frederic Henry Hedge.* Revised ed. New York: Octagon Books, 1972.

Wendte, Charles W. *The Wider Fellowship: Memories, Friendships, and Endeavors for Religious Unity, 1844-1927.* Two vols. Boston: Beacon Press, 1927.

Wilber, Earl Morse. *History of Unitarianism: Socinianism and Its Antecedents.* Cambridge: Harvard University Press, 1945.

_____. *Our Unitarian Heritage.* Boston: Beacon Press, 1925.

Williams, George H. et al. *The Harvard Divinity School: Its Place in Harvard University and in American Culture.* Boston: Beacon Press, 1954.

Woodhull, Victoria C. *The Principles of Social Freedom.* New York, 1872.

_____. *Tried as by Fire; or the True and the False Socially.* New York, 1874.

Wright, C. Conrad, ed. *The Liberal Christians: Essays on American Unitarian History.* Boston: Beacon Press, 1970.

_____, ed. *A Stream of Light: A Sesquicentennial History of American Unitarianism.* Boston: Unitarian Universalist Association, 1975.

INDEX

Abbot, Edward Stanley (brother of FEA), 5, 42, 153

Abbot, Edward Stanley (son of FEA), 43, 154

Abbot, Edwin, 2, 5, 11, 21, 33, 42

Abbot, Emily, 3, 5, 26, 37

Abbot, Fanny Ellingwood, 1-4, 21, 23, 153

Abbot, Francis Ellingwood: early life, 1-6; early religious influences, 3, 6-7; and John Randall, 6-8; Boston Latin School, 8-12; college life, 15-29; meets Katharine Loring, 17-19; conversion of, 20-25; as evangelical Unitarian, 25-26, 28, 31-32; decides to enter ministry, 28, 31-32; marriage and family life, 30, 33-34, 49, 131-33; at Harvard Divinity School, 32-34; at Meadville, 34-41; movement away from Christianity, 38-41, 44-45; scientific interests, 38-40; Unitarian ministry at Dover, 45-49; Free Religious ministry at Dover, 51-54; and Dover case, 54-55, 57, 60; and the "Battle of Syracuse," 66-69; formation of Free Religious Association, 69-73, 77-78; ministry at Toledo, 81-82, 84-87; and *Index*, 87-90, 91-99, 132-33; and secularism, 101-103, 109-11; and National Liberal League, 104-108, regarding Anthony Comstock, 115-19, 127; and the splitting of the National Liberal League, 120-25; withdrawal from public life, 128-29; and Harvard philosophers, 131, 134-35, 149-50; political views, 152-53; death of, 153-54

philosophy, 33, 44, 137-48, 149-50

religious views, 47-50, 51-52, 57, 71, 85, 91-95, 98-99, 101, 136-37, 151-52

Abbot, George, 1

Abbot, Henry, 2, 5, 21

Abbot, Joseph Hale, 1, 8, 153

Abbot, Katharine Loring, 17-26, 28, 30, 33-35, 37, 43, 132, 153

Abolitionism, 45, 110, 116, 126, 129; "mystique" of and Free Religion, 69, 74, 77, 152

Adams, Henry, 3, 9

Agassiz, Louis, 39

Agnosticism, 39-40, 141

Agricola, Johannes, 96

American Liberal Union. *See* National Liberal League of America

American Secular Union, 124

American Unitarian Association, 62, 65, 68, 86. *See also* National Unitarian Conference(s); Unitarianism

Andrews, Stephen Pearl, 90, 114-15

Anonyma Society (Harvard), 16, 19

Anti-Catholicism, in *Index,* 91, 92, 105, 106, 108

Anti-imperialism, 152

Anti-slavery. *See* Abolitionism

Antioch College, 62, 65, 68

Antisthenes, 142

Aristotle, 142-44

Augustine, Saint, 21

Bacon, Francis, 39, 140n

Baer, Ernst von, 39

Bain, Alexander, 140

Balch, Francis V., 26

Baltimore *Crucible. See Crucible* (Baltimore)

Banner of Light (Boston), 101-103

Barnes, Benjamin, Jr., 48, 53-54

Bartol, Cyrus A., 69-72, 131

Bayard, Thomas F., 110

Beecher, Henry W., 93, 113

Bellows, Henry W., 63-65, 67-68, 84-85

Bennett, D. M. (DeRobigne Mortimer), 97, 117-19, 124-25

Berkeley, George, 140

Besant, Annie, 115

Bible reading, opposed to in schools, 86, 92, 102-103, 108-109

Bissell, Edward, 83

Blackwell, Henry B., 71

Blaine, James G., 108, 152

Blanchard, Henry, 73

Blood, James H., 113

Boston *Banner of Light. See Banner of Light* (Boston)

Boston *Investigator. See Investigator* (Boston)

Boston Latin School, 2, 4, 8-12, 13

Bowen, Daniel, 81

Bowen, Francis, 134

Bradlaugh, Charles, 115, 125

British Secular Union, 125

Brooks, Phillips, 10

Brown, T. L. (Titus L.), 119, 121

Brown University, 29

Bryant, William Cullen, 15, 18, 22